GOLF
THE PASSION AND THE CHALLENGE

GOLF
THE PASSION AND THE CHALLENGE

by Mark Mulvoy and Art Spander
Special Photography by Ellen Griesedieck

A Rutledge Book
Published by Prentice-Hall, Inc.
Englewood Cliffs, N.J.

Publisher: Fred R. Sammis
Executive Director: John T. Sammis
Editor-in-Chief: Jeanne McClow
Art Director: Allan Mogel
Production Director: Julianne deVere
Editors: Jeremy Friedlander, Mimi Koren, B. G. Murphy
Associate Editors: Jay Hyams, Lee Hoeting
Associate Art Director: Elyse Shick
Art Associate: Eric Marshall
Editorial Assistants: Susan Lurie, Candida Pilla
Production Assistant: Lori Stein

Prepared and produced by Rutledge Books,
a division of Arcata Consumer Products Corporation.
Published in 1977 by Prentice-Hall, Inc.,
Englewood Cliffs, New Jersey
Copyright 1977 in all countries of the
International Copyright Union by Rutledge Books
and Prentice-Hall, Inc. All rights reserved.
Printed in Spain.

Library of Congress Cataloging in Publication Data
Mulvoy, Mark.
    Golf: the passion and the challenge.
    "A Rutledge book."
    1. Golf. I. Spander, Art joint author.
II. Title.
GV965.M74   796.352   76-53968
ISBN 0-13-357962-X

D. L. B. 18008-1977   Printer industria gráfica sa.
Tuset, 19 Barcelona   Sant Vicenç dels Horts 1977

Page 1: Tom Weiskopf; pages 2–3: sixth green of Torrey Pines North Course, San Diego, California; pages 6–7: Hale Irwin; pages 8–9: George Archer; pages 24–25: Thirteenth green, John's Island South Course, John's Island, Florida; pages 86–87: Scoreboard at the Jackie Gleason Inverrary Golf Tournament; pages 126–27: Johnny Miller; pages 162–63: Arnold Palmer; pages 192–93: Pebble Beach, Carmel, California; pages 210–211, left to right: Jack Nicklaus, Julius Boros, Gene Sarazen, Peter Thomson, Bobby Locke, Walter Hagen, Arnold Palmer, Sam Snead, Harry Vardon, Ben Hogan, Gary Player, Bobby Jones, Cary Middlecoff, Byron Nelson, Lee Trevino, Billy Casper.

CONTENTS

Golf is usually played with the outward appearance
of great dignity. It is nevertheless a game of
considerable passion, either of the explosive type,
or that which burns inwardly and sears the soul.

Bobby Jones

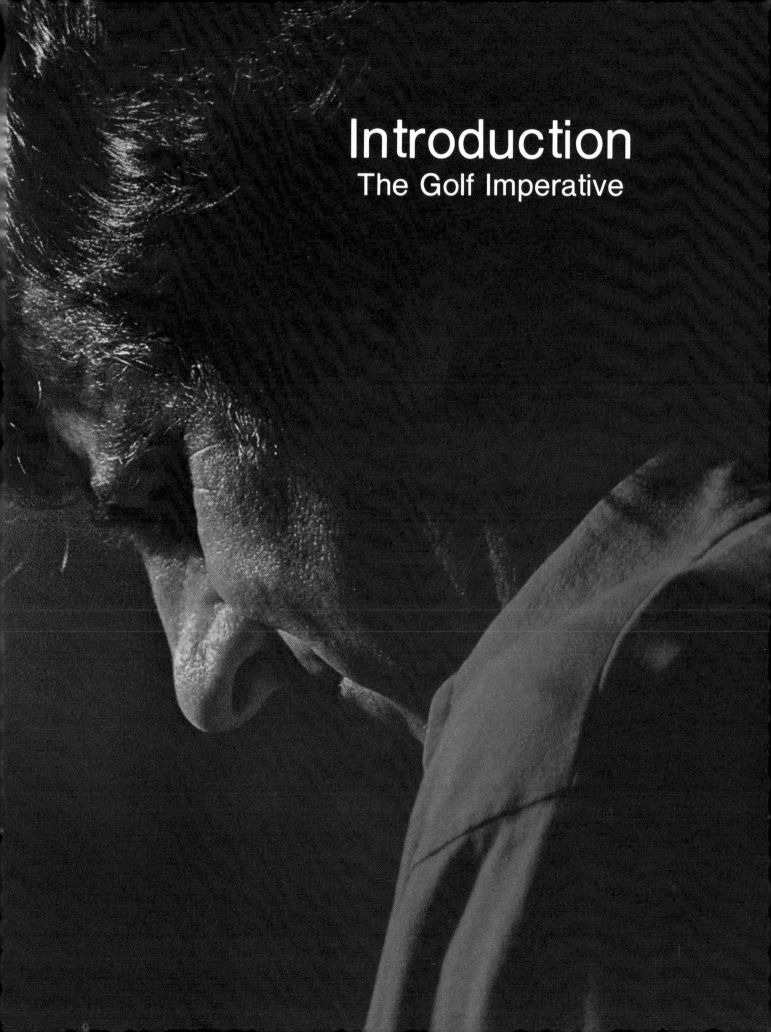

Introduction
The Golf Imperative

You are alone. You are in full control of your destiny. You can create a masterpiece or a muddle and there will be no one else to credit or blame but yourself.

No perfect pitches get belted out of the park. No short lobs get belted into the net. No perfect passes get dropped; no missed jump shots get tapped in. There are no opponents and no teammates who ruin or reprieve you. Just you.

You have all the time you need to do what you want and an impartial standard against which to measure yourself.

Are you ready? Anyone with money and courage can play. Money for the clubs, the clothes, the balls, the greens fees, the club dues. Courage for the confrontation with yourself. For golf is a game of individual achievements and failures. You face the challenge of the course alone; your teammate is the self-indulgent belief that you can beat it. Your opponent, in the last analysis, is yourself—your inadequacies, your poor judgment, your helplessness. Par is an immediate and unrelenting yardstick. You either play well or you don't, and your score leaves no room for doubt.

And what does it all prove—this genteel, slightly absurd ritual of, as a nineteenth-century logic tutor at Oxford put it, "putting little balls into little holes with instruments very ill-adapted to the purpose"? Just this: your worth. For golf is a game not just of manners but of morals. "Play it as it lies" is the first commandment: accept your fate and overcome it, if you can. Don't talk of the game's absurdity. That's not the point. A golfer finds out a great deal about himself during an 18-hole round, and besides, life itself could be regarded as an equally unwieldy venture. The fact is we must cope or cop out, and there is no finer place to learn that lesson than on the golf course. Whether your idea of coping is smelling the flowers as you go along or staring down the challenge of a three-foot character builder, golf allows you a chance to triumph over yourself. It's a game of the ego.

This challenge can be intimidating, and the game's trappings are often attempts to mitigate it. Consider, for example, the gentleman from Portland, Oregon, who shows up for his weekly round of golf wearing a shirt emblazoned with the logotype of the famous Doral Country Club in Miami. He hasn't played there, just visited to buy some conspicuous souvenirs. Pretentious? Perhaps. Or, put another way, it's a boost for the ever-faltering ego. If you can't conquer Doral, you can still dress as if you could. In golf the garb of the pros is not only accepted but expected from rank amateurs, not only copied but exaggerated. A bank president who barely permits himself a striped tie at work will appear on the course in blue and white polka-dot pants, an aquamarine shirt, and two-tone shoes. It's more than a little showing off. Those flashy clothes project an image of outrageous self-assurance for someone who needs all the self-assurance he can muster. Is it too much to suggest that such confidence may in fact be lacking and that the wild clothes are a means of bolstering it? Then what might have been a crash landing for the ego becomes only a bumpy one, the golfer having assured himself with his sporty clothes that he is sport enough to accept the verdict of the golf course, however harsh.

Clothes are not the only palliative for the cruelty of golf. Next to a full backswing and a smooth putting stroke, the excuse may be the most cultivated part of the game. Even the most proficient golfers, the touring pros, have a stockpile of excuses: the sun was in their eyes; the wind came up unexpectedly; they misread the yardage; the caddie gave them the wrong club; their spikes slipped; breakfast didn't agree with them; the sand in the bunkers was too soft, or too coarse; even—indeed—the grass grew too quickly. (The last excuse, a little contrived if not entirely untrue, is to be used only as a last resort, in major tournaments. It exploits the fact that the

The theatrics of the game—clockwise from top left: JoAnne Carner playing to the gallery; Susie McAllister, lady in waiting; Ben Crenshaw radiating a happy ending; Raymond Floyd on the fringe.

11

grass, after it is trimmed by the greenskeeper early in the morning, will grow a fraction of an inch on a sunny day. Thus, putting speed on the greens decreases. Moreover, the grass on the fairway may poke between clubface and ball and create a flying lie—the absence of backspin that is usually imparted by the grooves of the club.)

P. G. Wodehouse went so far as to create a character, ostensibly fictional, who whined about missing short putts because of the uproar butterflies made in an adjoining meadow.

When excuses pale, the golfer in search of success may be reduced to a temper tantrum. In other sports you can purge your frustrations by crashing into an opponent. Golf has no place for such catharsis; it is supposed to be a sport of decorum, of well-dressed men and women in a genteel atmosphere. And yet to the intemperate amateur this veneer of civility is hardly a deterrent. A favorite poster in many pro shops depicts an Oriental tourist musing, "I just come from America, where I learn about game called Ah Shit."

"Terrible Tempered" Tommy Bolt was the patron saint of such duffers. One day Bolt had a 350-yard shot to a green and asked for his three-wood. The caddie handed him a three-iron. Cursing darkly, Bolt demanded the wood again, insisting that no one would use an iron from that distance. The caddie shrugged helplessly. It was the only club he had left, he explained, except for a putter, and Bolt had broken the handle off that earlier in the round. In his later years Bolt claimed that many of the stories about him were contrived. But the evidence against him was compelling when *Sports Illustrated* ran a two-picture sequence from the 1960 U.S. Open at Cherry Hills in Denver, showing Bolt hitting a tee shot into a lake and then immediately hurling the club into the water. (A young boy dived in, retrieved the club, and handed it to a rather contrite Bolt, who mumbled his thanks.)

In the 1960s, apparently in an attempt to improve its image, the Professional Golfers' Association (PGA) instituted an automatic fine for club throwing and club breaking. Then, modifying its edict as if to admit that a small show of temper was only natural, it ruled that no fine would be levied if the golfer kept hold of both sections of the club on breaking it.

Lefty Stackhouse, who played the pro tour in the 1930s and early 1940s, would treat various parts of his body as if they were independent beings and apportion them responsibility for his errors. One day Lefty hit a bad hook and immediately

The cheery dashes of color (above, left) *can't cloak the rather grim reality that golf can be a desolate experience,* opposite.

concluded that the trouble had been caused by his right hand turning over on the shot. "Take that!" he shouted, as he slapped the hand violently against a tree trunk. Stackhouse is the man who once attempted to strangle his putter and once after missing a short putt battered the club against the radiator of his car. Ky Laffoon was known to have plunged his putter into a lake and screamed, "Drown you son of a bitch, drown!"

Writer H. L. Mencken fumed, "If I had my way a man guilty of golf would be ineligible for any public office in the United States, and the families

of the breed would be shipped off to the white slave corrals of the Argentine." But as Bolt and his fellow sufferers demonstrate, golf might be more accurately described as the punishment rather than the crime. The Scots, who invented the pastime, even theorized that the Almighty had provided golf to make man suffer and then bestowed Scotch whiskey on him to ease the pain.

Such quips bring to mind that other great salve of the golfer—humor, particularly black humor. A few years ago, so the story goes, a lawyer and his friend were playing at a course in West Los

A precarious existence. Above: *Joe Brown searches for a way out.* Opposite: *Ron Ely on tilt.*

Angeles, and the friend sliced his tee shot into a road next to the third hole. The ball crashed through the windshield of an oncoming car and struck the driver, knocking him unconscious and causing the vehicle to run into a fence. Understandably upset, the man who had hit the ball turned to his lawyer/playing partner and asked, "What do you think I should do?" Whereupon the counselor advised, "Well, I'd turn the right hand under a little more and . . ."

A few years ago a golf magazine included a drawing of a skeleton lying in a clump of bushes next to a fairway, the bones of one hand wrapped around a golf club. A golfer standing nearby was thoughtfully regarding the macabre sight and telling his caddie, "You can't get out of this stuff with an eight-iron, apparently. Give me a wedge."

Sporty clothes, elaborate excuses, temper tantrums, black humor—all attempts to compensate for the cruelty of the game. Indeed the entire scenic and social setting of golf seems to fulfill a similar function. For the most part golf is a sport played in a very controlled, pretty setting. Nature has been tamed into a garden, the players into strolling garden partygoers. Studied casualness surrounds, almost obscures, the very intense contest. (To nongolfers this nonchalance often seems to *be* the game—golf as a social event rather than a sport.)

Logically enough, the golfer wants a soothing environment for his struggle. If you're going to undertake an ordeal of self-examination and testing, it may as well be amid pretty meadows and glades, and among companions who, presumably, are your friends. Ascetics may argue that it is more efficient to face up to the stark reality of yourself in a stark setting. But most of us prefer more gentle confrontations.

And so the intimidation of golf, the stark challenge to the individual that lies at the root of the game, is cloaked in reassuring blandishments with a quite different lure. Here is a sport that

almost anyone is physically capable of playing—men, women, and children, big and small, fit and fat. It offers physical exercise that, if no more strenuous than mowing the lawn or cleaning the attic, is at least more pleasant. How intimidating could such a do-able sport be?

The addicted golfer knows, since he has faced the formidable challenge of this game beneath its gentle accessibility. He experiences the game not just as a pastime but as an imperative. It is to him that the passion of golf reveals itself, and in him (and his eccentricities) that one finds the basic and most powerful lure of the game.

Journalist and television commentator Alistair Cooke came upon the game at middle age, shot 168 in his first round, and immediately became addicted. He calls golf, "an open exhibition of overweening ambition, courage deflated by stupidity, skill soured by a whiff of arrogance. . . . These humiliations are the essence of the game."

If golfers do not enjoy such pain and thus are not simply masochists, it does seem that they thirst for the discipline that inevitably produces pain. Golf is a kind of purgatory. It makes compelling demands on the golfer to confront himself, and as he acts on these demands, he experiences both pain and redemption. The game stimulates the player. But it is only a stimulus; it can itself be conquered no more than can life, that other purgatory.

Start with the swing, probably the single most important motion in sports. If it is right, the journey from tee to green becomes as easy as calculating distances and compensating for wind (tricky, but rarely as complicated as repairing an imperfect swing). And so the swing is endlessly scrutinized and analyzed. Every day sports pages across the country carry sidebar instructions from the ghostwriters of Arnold Palmer, Jack Nicklaus, Lee Trevino, and Billy Casper. Aim the thumbs to the left, to the right; pull the left foot back from the

Top: *Golden John Miller in repose.* Above: *Amy Alcott tenses to turn loose.* Opposite: *Gary Player suspended in disbelief.*

line of flight; pull the right foot back; cock the wrists at the top of the swing; don't cock the wrists. Golfers absorb this advice reverently and diligently practice swinging everywhere—in elevators, meeting rooms, cocktail lounges, airports, even on television—as if serenity itself is to be found in constantly repeating the swing, like some chant. It soon transcends a mechanical motion and becomes a state of mind—ideally no longer a matter of straightened elbows or bent knees but of a tranquil, creative spirit, from which it will spring untroubled automatically.

Michael Murphy, author, cofounder of the Esalen Institute for behavioral science research, and student of the one-piece swing, calls golf the ultimate form of meditation. On the other hand, George Plimpton, whimsical writer and pedestrian duffer, hypothesized that while he is swinging, miniature beings are screaming instructions through megaphones from his brain to the muscles of the arms and legs. That turbulent condition, he recognized, produces equally turbulent swings.

But whether you meditate to transcendent calm or you fantasize to writhing neurosis, the game of golf remains unmoved by the game it moves you to play within yourself. Par is still par, the sand traps don't move, the fairways don't expand or contract. An unexpectedly bad lie here or a good one there is bestowed with, all in all, fairly random chance. Whether you're playing well or poorly, the game treats you impartially.

Not so other sports. In football, if your team is playing well and the opposition poorly, an 80-yard touchdown drive can be a carefree romp. If you're playing poorly and the opposition well, a 1-yard plunge can be a forced march. Other games are only what the interaction of opponents makes them. Golf is that and more—independent, indomitable.

It is indomitable too because it is so varied. Each course teaches the game differently. Other sports strive for similar if not always uniform playing fields, in size, composition, and condition.

The trouble with trouble in golf is that you are almost invariably to blame for it. Here, Hale Irwin tries to cope.

18

Golf celebrates variety, from booming par fives to petite par threes, from alligator-infested water hazards to sagebrush rough. It is almost as if the course is the game, and therefore each different course a different game. Golfers speak of "playing" Pebble Beach, or Oakmont, or Merion as if to say simply "playing golf" is meaningless. (Indeed in the case of courses such as Pebble Beach, where conditions fluctuate wildly, it is not enough to identify the course. You pretty well have to append a weather report if you want to convey what sort of game you were playing.) To conquer golf one would have to conquer all the different courses.

One Nathan Tufts considered the conquest of a course no more than surviving its 18 holes, and in 1970 he announced his intention to play 300 rounds of golf that year, one each on 300 different American courses. A kindred spirit, Alfred Vlautin, of San Francisco, set himself the goal in life of playing every course in northern California. He tacked a map to a wall in his home and marked with pins the location of 160 courses. In time each pin was replaced with a black dot—mission accomplished. "I had to work to get on some of the private courses," Vlautin recalled with more than a hint of pride in his voice, "but I've played them all."

Some time later, Vlautin read of a hole-in-one at a local course he had never heard of. Badly shaken, he called to find out about it. He learned, to his relief, that he did know the course after all (and he had played it)—it had existed for years but had recently changed its name. Grateful but still disconcerted, he managed a few words of thanks.

Asked why he wanted to play all those courses, Vlautin responded with a mountain climber's sense of conquest, "Because they're there."

Bizarre? Not compared to the two intrepid souls who took it upon themselves to play courses that weren't there. In the summer of 1974, teenagers Bob Aube and Phil Marrone played the four

hundred miles from San Francisco (starting at Harding Park) to Los Angeles (ending at the Bel Air Country Club) in a mere 16 days and an estimated five hundred thousand shots.

Even allowing for the publicity gimmickry of these ventures, one can begin to appreciate a golf course's hold on a golfer. A round can be leisurely or intense, sociable or hostile, depending on the players, but to a great extent the course determines the atmosphere. You just don't feel the same playing Doral's Blue Monster as you do some cozy, familiar, gentle par 70 back home. And you haven't fully enjoyed the game until you have experienced its different settings. It takes only an appreciation of the game's possibilities, not some misguided notion of symbolic conquest or a craving for publicity to want to embark on a golf odyssey.

The urge gripped Alan Shepard on February 6, 1971, when he plunked down a golf ball on the moon, shortly after arriving there himself, and proceeded to go to work with his six-iron. Restricted by his space suit, he missed with his first swing. "I said a few unprintable words under my breath," he confessed, "and called it a Mulligan." His next effort sent the little ball soaring through the nonresistant lunar atmosphere some two hundred yards straight down the fairway, the highlands of Fra Mauro. (As a reward for that caper, Shepard was invited to the 1972 Bing Crosby Pro-Am Tournament.)

Whether or not you are charmed by teenagers bashing a golf ball down Highway 101 or by an astronaut wafting them over the lunar surface, it's hard to ignore the golfer's impossible yet irrepressible dream to concoct and conquer the ultimate golf challenge. It is as if there is something reassuring to many golfers about this indomitability of their game. They seem pleased to rediscover it continually, to be continually reminded of their inadequacy. "There is a certain romance in futility pursued," actor Efrem

Zimbalist, Jr., an avid golfer, observed about golf. It is the romance of bringing some green monster to its knees or of virtually falling to one's knees in reverence before it. Either way, the game is implacable, offering its lessons like some inexhaustible discipline of nature—the mountains or the seas. "A golfer always loses on the golf course," concluded Zimbalist, with no indication that it should ever be otherwise. Purgatory is demanding but cleansing.

One can even become honest at golf. In other sports, honesty is the referee's problem. Players do not readily admit to fouls or penalties when called for them and would not think of volunteering incriminating evidence that the ref has missed. Innocent until caught red-handed. In golf, for the most part there is no Big Brother watching, which gives you a chance to be the ref yourself. Power corrupts, it is said, but it has also been known to ennoble. Vested with the responsibility of calling the shots, even if they are his own, a golfer can become scrupulous. In the 1925 U.S. Open, to cite the most famous example, Bobby Jones nudged his ball while addressing it on the eleventh hole and called the penalty stroke on himself, though no one would have noticed had he failed to. That honorable act cost him the tournament (he fell into

a tie with Willie Macfarlane and lost the playoff), but Jones showed no regret. "There is nothing to talk about, and you are not to write about it," he admonished newsmen, who were eager to work a little saintliness into their stories. "There is only one way to play the game."

You don't have to be quite that high-minded and moralistic to appreciate the rewards of honorable golf, to understand that it can be more satisfying to play a ball in the rough than to kick it out. Somehow, simple decency isn't as compelling in other sports. In golf it's easier to break the rules, but it's more rewarding to follow them, which may be part of the reason why the honor system survives.

Then there are the aesthetic fringe benefits of this discipline called golf. It was mentioned above that nature functions on a golf course to soothe the beleaguered player. But then too, it can inspire the tranquil one. Many a golfer has awakened on a beautiful morning, longed to go golfing for no reason other than that the golf course is an ideal place to appreciate a fine morning, and discovered the happy coincidence that the smells and sights of nature working its wonders can infuse one's game with a wonder-working spirit.

It's a bit difficult to pin down, of course. Who

Birds of paradise—horticultural, above right; *human,* above. Opposite: *Paradise.*

knows whether those pros who stop to look at the brilliantly blooming azaleas behind the thirteenth green at the Augusta National are moved to brilliance on account of it? But the proper functioning of the body is often a sensual process (athletes are continually talking about how they feel), and a golf course abounds in richly sensual stimuli: the exquisite delicacy of dew on the greens, the perfume of freshly cut grass, the chill of a late-afternoon breeze. It's hard to visualize a player sensually impressed by such things who isn't able to feel how his body is functioning. And once he is in touch with what he is doing, it's a lot easier to do it right.

Suddenly, the pressure of golf all but dissolves, as the game ceases to be an internal test of the will and the other synthetics of the mind. It becomes a physical harmony, the golfer at peace with himself if not precisely at one with his surroundings. He plays serenely, expending great mental and physical energy without strain. Golf is no longer purgatory, just pleasure.

This is that exalted state, common to most sports, when the unsuspecting player sees everything going right and thinks he has conquered the game, when in fact he has only untangled himself. Foolishly, he begins to imagine the ideal, lucky game, over which he really has no control—60-foot putts dropping, pin-high approach shots stopping dead on the green. He fantasizes about the results of shots instead of continuing to concentrate on making the shots. Then a well-stroked putt unaccountably stays out or a solid drive finds a bad lie and he wonders whether the magic is gone. Soon his self-doubts are alive and well again, and he's back in purgatory, trying to confront and conquer them anew.

Playing golf well is not an elusive, ephemeral state of grace. But being lucky may very well be.

You're well on your way toward coping with golf when you can tell the difference. Then you enjoy the exhilaration of good luck without getting intoxicated (losing touch with your game) and saddling yourself with a hangover when your luck turns sour. Being in a slump is a mental problem of not truly knowing what you can do. And there's no quicker way to get there than to mistake good luck for skill, because then bad luck inevitably seems to you to be a lack of skill.

If it's any consolation, many a pro has fallen out of touch with his game. After joining the tour in 1964, George Archer won an average of $77,000 a year for nine years. Then in the next three years he won less than $30,000 a year. "It's mass confusion," he moaned after one difficult day. "I'm guessing on every shot. About the only thing left for me is acupuncture in the brain."

At least Archer recognized where the problem lay. Many players, slumping and otherwise, will do anything to escape the conclusion that they are the cause (and the cure) of their problems. They swap up miracle remedies almost indiscriminately, so firm is their faith in self-helplessness.

We've come full circle—from the intimidating loneliness and purgative challenge, to the achievements of self-awareness, to the false paradise of good luck, to the self-doubts bred of failure. Then back to loneliness and challenge. Somehow golfers seem to be able to pick themselves up and start again.

We'll resist the urge to make of this pattern any more than a golf life cycle, and close simply by noting its consonance with the remarkable regenerative power of all species. Anyone wishing to pursue the investigation further is invited to make a field trip before dawn to any municipal course in or around a metropolitan center. There, in the darkness, he will come upon golfers stirring quietly, not yet quite awake, waiting to rise again.

The quest begins again. If he is hardy enough to play at
dawn but not so hardened as to follow only his ball,
a golfer can appreciate the other beauties of a new day.

1
Sculpting the Land
The Making of a Golf Course

It is obviously the function of the championship course to present competitors with a variety of problems that will test every type of shot which a golfer of championship ability should be qualified to play. Thus, it should call for long and accurate tee shots, accurate iron play (and let me say here that I consider the ability to play the longer irons as the supreme test of a great golfer), precise handling of the short game and, finally, consistent putting. These abilities should be called for in a proportion that will not permit excellence in any one department of the game to too-largely offset deficiencies in another. Likewise, penalties should not be unduly severe nor of a nature that will prohibit a full recovery by the execution of an unusually well-played shot. These are the problems presented to the golf architect when undertaking the design of a championship layout.

With those words, Donald Ross, who created many of the greatest golf courses in the United States during the first half of the twentieth century, gave the neophyte golf architects of the world—everyone, it seems, from Jack Nicklaus to Arnold Palmer, Jackie Gleason to Glen Campbell—a basic primer for golf course design. Unfortunately, however, too many of the modern-day architects have failed to follow the instructions of Mr. Ross closely enough. In fact, of today's architects, only Nicklaus, the accomplished Pete Dye, Joe Lee, and, at times, George Fazio and Robert Trent Jones have preserved the elegance and standards of the past in their work. Most new courses in the United States today might have qualified as highways in the days when Ross, Charles Blair MacDonald, Alister MacKenzie, Hugh Wilson, A. W. Tillinghast, Perry Maxwell, Henry C. Fownes, and Dick Wilson, among others, were creating such grand courses as Seminole, the National Golf Links, Augusta National, Merion, Winged Foot, Prairie Dunes,

Oakmont, Cypress Point, and Pinehurst Number 2.

In fairness to these modern movers of the earth, it should be mentioned that occasionally they and their designs have been innocent victims of the great golf boom in the United States. Over the past fifteen years the demand for new golf courses has been so heavy that architects have been forced to turn out their designs almost on photocopying machines, using one grand master schematic for all their courses regardless of the particular topographical features of each site. Back in 1950, there were fewer than 5,000 golf courses in the United States. In 1960, there were almost 6,400 courses, an increase of almost 30 percent. And by 1975, as Americans by the millions discovered golf, there were more than 12,300 grounds for the country's divot diggers and designs for hundreds more on the drawing boards and in the photocopiers.

During the period from 1960 to 1975, the basic purpose of golf course construction changed quite drastically. In the days of Ross, Tillinghast, and MacKenzie, golf courses were strictly the architect's creation—one man's vision of a suitable, distinctive challenge to golfers. Nowadays, as part of a national trend most closely associated with the work of Robert Trent Jones (whom golf writer Herbert Warren Wind has called "the Howard Johnson of golf architects"), most new golf courses are packaged as part of land development projects, hotel resort complexes, and retirement villages. The developers and the hotel operators use their "championship" golf course, as all these layouts are labeled, to attract home buyers and vacationers. The architect is left to work under conditions that restrict him from producing his best results. For one thing, the land-development specialists, carefully guided by the directives of their financial sponsors, rarely permit the golf architects to use the best parcels of land for their course layouts. Instead, they keep the best property to use for homes, condominiums,

Pebble Beach represents a long-lost era when the choicest plots of land were available to golf course architects. Exploiting this setting to the fullest, architects Jack Neville and Douglas Grant fashioned a marvelously diverse course. It can be serene, left; spectacular, below; and, of course, extremely treacherous, below left.

The designs of the prolific modern-day architect, Robert Trent Jones, range from challenging to tormenting to pampering. The mammoth South Course at Firestone Country Club in Akron, Ohio, belongs to the first category (below, *the eighteenth hole*); Dorado Beach in Puerto Rico (left *and* opposite) *to the last.*

beach clubs, marinas, and hotels, and give the golf architect simply the leftovers.

Pebble Beach, probably the finest golf course in North America, occupies a rich piece of property on Carmel Bay above the Pacific Ocean. Eight of the holes at Pebble Beach are on the water, and the eighteenth hole, set on a cliff overlooking the bay, may just be the most spectacular golf hole and the most spectacular piece of real estate in the world. Pebble Beach was laid out in 1919. It is safe to say that if its architects, Jack Neville and Douglas Grant, had done the project in, oh, 1967, when golf was in the middle of its smashing boom, there would be homes and condominiums spread along the ocean and the bay, and the golf course would be set inland, far from the water.

The first golf course architect was a 15-handicapper with a whippy swing from Scotland named Father Nature. It's a long and rather involved tale, so here are just the basics. The first golf courses were set on the linksland that naturally formed around the shores of Great Britain when the seas receded after the Ice Age and left huge deposits of rich sand. Birds fertilized the links and eventually grass, gorse, heather, and a variety of other vegetation began to grow. Later, sheep, rabbits, and human beings started to wear paths through the linksland, and these paths became what we now call fairways. Driving places were set out; cup holes were dug.

As time passed and the demand for golf courses spread through Great Britain, the British and the Scots produced some masterful architects, including Herbert Fowler, H. S. Colt, Tom Simpson, James Braid, and J. H. Taylor. The United States, which discovered golf around the mid-1870s, began to produce its own school of golf course architects, starting with Charles Blair MacDonald. A former student at a school near St. Andrews in Scotland, MacDonald revisited many of the great Scottish links before he designed America's first great course, the National Golf Links on Great

The mass products of Robert Trent Jones, above, often lack the craftsmanship that the old master, Donald Ross, top, brought to these two greens, at Pinehurst Number 2 (opposite top) and Scioto (opposite bottom). The subtle contouring and pronounced bunkering convey Ross's stress on accuracy over distance.

Peconic Bay at Southampton, far out on New York's Long Island, around the turn of the century. While MacDonald favored the Scottish-links style of golf architecture, Donald Ross introduced Americans to a new design concept.

A native of Scotland, Ross settled around Pinehurst, North Carolina, in the late 1890s. Ross was masterfully subtle, his designs featuring well-contoured greens and strategically placed bunkers and trees. He was an advocate of accuracy and placement, not length. He wrote, "The contours and slopes of the greens are used to break up the greens so that the player near the cup has an opportunity for one putt while the golfer whose play to the green has been less than accurate does not have that same opportunity." Ross created some of America's finest courses, among them Pinehurst Number 2; Inverness in Toledo; Oak Hill in Rochester; Oakland Hills outside Detroit; Seminole in North Palm Beach; and Scioto in Columbus, Ohio, the course on which Jack Nicklaus learned to play the game.

Hugh Wilson obviously shared some of Ross's thoughts about golf course architecture, for in creating Merion, off the Main Line of Philadelphia, he ignored sheer length in favor of a fairly short (less than 6,500 yards) layout designed to challenge golfers with its subtleties. Before building Merion, Wilson spent almost a year overseas studying the great courses in Great Britain, with the result that Merion has distinctly British and Scottish overtones. In setting out Merion, Wilson laid white bed sheets on the ground to plot the location of the bunkers and then moved the sheets around to satisfy his fancies. There are some one hundred and fifty bunkers at Merion, and they are called, after Wilson's bed sheets, "the White Faces of Merion."

George Crump was more sadistic than Wilson and Ross. He created a treacherous challenge in building Pine Valley in Clementon, New Jersey, the most difficult course in North America, if not in the

world. Set among sand, scrub, water, and even some patches of grass, Pine Valley is target golf at its best. There is usually one place and only one place to hit a shot at Pine Valley, and if you don't hit the shot to that one place, you might never find the golf ball again. Pine Valley was—and despite women's lib probably still is—a bastion of male chauvinism; in fact, when newlywed Jack Nicklaus decided to interrupt his honeymoon to test the course he had heard so much about, he had to leave his wife, Barbara, waiting in their car at the entrance gate for the four or so hours it took him

to experience the horrors of Pine Valley.

Henry C. Fownes must have shared Crump's distaste for green grass, for in building Oakmont, outside Pittsburgh, Fownes seemed to place sand traps where the grass should have been. All told, Fownes used more than two hundred bunkers for the course, including the treacherous Church Pews. All were raked to make escape a feat. Even modern architects, whose idea of challenging a golfer can be to crucify him, admit that Oakmont extracts too much blood from its visitors.

A. W. Tillinghast, whose works included Winged Foot and Baltusrol, two regular U.S. Open sites

Alister MacKenzie in consultation with Bobby Jones designed the famous Augusta National course, home of the Masters Tournament. Opposite: Looking beyond the fourth and sixth greens to the sixteenth hole, par three over water. Above right: Thirteenth green and adjacent fourteenth tee.

within a forty-five minute drive (in opposite directions) of New York City, generally favored rather long courses, and at the same time he protected his greens, which were usually elevated a bit, with deep greenside bunkers or thick, wiry rough. If you miss a Tillinghast green, there is little chance you will be able to save your par.

America's most surprising golf course is deep in the heartland of the country, the land of the battered pick-up truck and the '49 Ford coupe, where a leisure suit is a T-shirt and tattered jeans. To get to the course, you roll into downtown Hutchinson, Kansas, take Thirtieth Street north to Route 35, turn east on Route 35, and stop past the "Slow School" sign. That's Prairie Dunes, more than a thousand miles from the closest ocean yet able to pass for one of those old Scottish links along the Irish Sea. Dunes in middle America? Yes, the dunes of Prairie Dunes in Hutchinson, Kansas, of all places, are the real thing. Dan Jenkins, famous golf writer for *Sports Illustrated,* once explained that the severe and constant winds that blow hard across the nearby Arkansas River probably built up the dunes just as sea breezes build them along a seacoast. Perry Maxwell, the architect who later created Southern Hills down in Tulsa, brought Scotland to Hutchinson by converting the links of Prairie Dunes into one of the toughest short courses (only 6,379 yards) in America. For added effect, Maxwell left the yucca plants in Prairie Dunes's bunkers. The wind blows constantly, and the course is so difficult that Jack Nicklaus has never scored better than 71, one over par, in his dozen or more visits.

Another versatile architect was Alister MacKenzie, the Scotsman who with the help of Bobby Jones designed Augusta National on the old Fruitlands nursery in Augusta, Georgia, and also laid out the great Cypress Point course, which is about a drive and a four-iron from Pebble Beach on the Monterey Peninsula in California. MacKenzie's sixteenth hole at Cypress, a 233-yard

Scotland in Kansas, otherwise known as Prairie Dunes. Perry Maxwell fashioned one of America's most distinctive courses from a most unusual landscape. Above right: Heathlike ground separates tee from green on tenth hole. Top right: Gorse nestles the second green. Above left: Good old American oak.

par three, is probably the most photographed and most discussed hole in golf. The tee shot must carry across the Pacific to a green that sits on a promontory and is surrounded by disaster. Normally, performing this delicate operation calls for a wood, but when the wind is up, nothing short of a guided missile will suffice. Henry Ransom quit Cypress Point in disgust one day after he failed to get his ball onto the green from the beach, some one hundred and fifty feet down a sheer cliff, where enormous rocks, ice plants, some seals, and other wildlife keep the golfer company. Ransom picked up after his sixteenth swing.

Enter, now, Robert Trent Jones, not to be confused with Robert Tyre Jones, the legendary amateur golfer who later turned architectural helper, aiding MacKenzie with Augusta National and the other R. T. Jones with Peachtree in Atlanta. To his credit, Robert Trent Jones has built or redesigned some of the finest courses in America, including the Firestone Country Club in Akron, Peachtree, Bellerive in St. Louis, and Pauma Valley in California. However, he also has constructed some of the country's most extreme layouts, where luck, not skill, seems to be the prevailing factor in a competition. For example, at the Jones-designed Hazeltine Club in Chaska, Minnesota, Britain's Tony Jacklin won the 1970 U.S. Open by a wide margin because Nicklaus, Palmer, and others of their ilk repeatedly flirted with scores in the eighties. Spyglass Hill, a catastrophe not far from Cypress Point in California, Mauna Kea in Hawaii, and the Dunes Club in Myrtle Beach, South Carolina, are some Jones courses seemingly designed to torment the skilled and unskilled indiscriminately. At the other extreme, in his role as a pioneer of the land development style of golf course, Jones has designed courses such as Dorado Beach in Puerto Rico that cater to a clientele not particularly eager to be challenged. Jones, incidentally, is such an advocate of dogleg holes (Mauna Kea, for

The sixteenth at Cypress Point, Alister MacKenzie's most spectacular creation, leaves the golfer on the tee defenseless against the elements.

example, has almost a dozen doglegs) that the pros like to joke that his corporate symbol ought to be the hind leg of a St. Bernard.

During the last decade America's leading golf professionals have hung their architect's shingles and collaborated with land development money men on hundreds of golf projects. Jackie Burke, Jr., and Jimmy Demaret helped create 36 exceptional holes at the Champions Club outside Houston, and Jack Nicklaus helped Pete Dye in the development of the Harbour Town Links at Hilton Head Island, South Carolina. Nicklaus also personally supervised the design of the new Memorial Course at the Muirfield Village Club in his hometown of Columbus, naming the club after Muirfield in Scotland, where Jack won his first British Open Championship in 1966. Some critics insist that Muirfield, Ohio, is the best course for play since Harbour Town. George Fazio, a semiretired pro who once lost a U.S. Open playoff to Ben Hogan at Merion, has designed two strong new courses: Butler National, a monster track on the outskirts of Chicago, and Jupiter Hills, a tough but not unfair layout on some dunesland in Jupiter, Florida, up the road from Seminole. (Jupiter Hills is probably the only hilly golf course in Florida.) Ben Hogan also has turned to golf architecture, overseeing the design for the Trophy Club's 36-hole layout near Fort Worth that, according to the few people who saw the layout during construction, will perfectly reflect Hogan's attitudes about how the game should be played. If Hogan comes even close to matching the late Dick Wilson's superb Pine Tree in Delray Beach, golfers will have a treat.

Of all the current architects, the one who seems to have had the strongest impact on the game from the standpoint of sheer genius as a creator is Pete Dye, who built Harbour Town with the help of Nicklaus, golf writer Charles Price, and even Dye's wife, Alice, who is one of the best amateur golfers in the United States and has played on a number of Curtis Cup teams. Dye's other credits include such great courses as Cajuiles, at La Romana, the Dominican Republic; Crooked Stick, in Indianapolis; The Golf Club, outside Columbus; and both courses at John's Island in Vero Beach, Florida. Unlike so many of today's architects, Dye has not been afraid to borrow ideas from the great architects, including even old Father Nature, of golf's early days. His courses all reflect the character of the land he is working with. According to his critics or, if you wish, his rivals, Dye is too much of an iconoclast to be a good designer. According to Dye, his rivals are not creative enough. "You don't create golf courses with a computer," Dye said. "You work a golf course with your hands, like they did in the old days, until you create what you want to create—if you want a real golf course, that is."

Pete Dye is a jolly-faced Midwesterner approaching fifty years of age who always wears black Gucci loafers and thinks the Miami Dolphins are the only football team in the world. He picked up his visitor in West Palm Beach, Florida, set his Cadillac on automatic pilot, pointed it north in the direction of John's Island, and started to talk about golf course architecture. "My dad was a five- or six-handicap golfer," Dye said, "and in the late 1920s and early 1930s he became interested in golf course construction in a rather roundabout way. My mother owned some farmland in Urbana, Ohio, and my father suggested that the land be turned into a golf course. He tried to get Donald Ross and some other architects to lay out a course, but they were all too busy. So he studied their designs and, in the end, built a nine-hole course that I still think is second to none, a fine up-and-down, goat-hill type of course."

Young Pete Dye grew up more or less with a five-iron in his hands, but after World War II he went straight and started an insurance business in Indianapolis. "I was the youngest life member of the million dollar roundtable," Dye said. "Believe me, I had one helluva business. All the time I was in the insurance business, though, I fussed around with golf course maintenance and design. For a long time I was a member of the U.S. Golf Association's greens committee. I fooled around with architecture the same way my father had. Then, in 1959, a friend of mine called me and said he wanted to turn four hundred acres of his farm into a golf course. 'Get me an architect, will you,' he said to me. Well, I called Dick Wilson, Robert Trent Jones, and six or seven others, but they were all busy. So I called my friend—he was a farmer named McLain—and told him that I had struck out." Dye paused.

"The next day McLain called me back and said, 'Why don't you come down and help me lay out this course?' I put down the phone, thought about his offer for thirty-seven seconds, called my wife, and made a major decision. I went to the office and told them I was taking the summer off to build a golf course.

"Let me tell you, we literally dug and shoveled and picked that course. I wanted to create a utopia. I wanted to have a USGA-approved sub-base for all the greens. I wanted perfect irrigation. Everything. Trouble was, ol' Mr. McLain didn't have that kind of money. We got the course done, and in September I went back to my office, ready to play insurance man once again. I looked at the people sitting at their desks, then shook my head, walked out, went home, and said to my wife, Alice, 'I can't go back.' She knew what I meant. I called the man who ran the insurance company and told him to send an auditor, that I was quitting the insurance business to become a golf architect. The man laughed at me. He said, 'Pete, before I send the auditor, I'll send you a psychiatrist.' No matter, I was out of the business. And after that, I got lucky right away.

"Dr. Harlan Hatcher, a Scotsman who was the president of the University of Michigan at Ann

Pete Dye at Cajuiles, the golf course he designed in La Romana, the Dominican Republic. His other credits include Harbour Town Links, in Hilton Head, South Carolina, and both John's Island courses, in Vero Beach, Florida.

Arbor, was searching for an architect to create a new university course on some prime land that an alumnus had left to the school, along with five hundred thousand dollars to cover the construction costs. The golf coach at Michigan was a friend of mine, and he suggested my name to Dr. Hatcher. Here I had built only two nine-hole courses in my life and because of the war I had not even graduated from high school, and now I was meeting with the president of the University of Michigan. At the time I had just returned from a visit to Scotland, where I had played and studied all the great courses. Anyway, I walked into Dr. Hatcher's office at 10 A.M. and walked out at 12:30 P.M. Dr. Hatcher's secretary said to me, 'Young man, I don't know who you are or where you're from, but as long as I've been Dr. Hatcher's secretary, nobody, including President Eisenhower, ever has spent more than half an hour in his office. And you were in with him for two and a half hours.' Dr. Hatcher called a few days later and offered me the job of building the new course, a 'Scottish-type course,' he said. Well, I built the course, and it's a good golf course. I'm not hanging my head, believe me, but I'd like to do that course now, on that same piece of great land, with the knowledge I have today.''

When Dye finished at Ann Arbor, he built The Golf Club outside Columbus in the early 1960s. ''Most architects build five and six courses at a time, hopping from one layout to another,'' Dye said, ''but I spent almost two full years at The Golf Club, contouring and positioning everything myself. I had almost finished the job, and one day Nicklaus came out to inspect the course. I knew Jack. In fact, I had played against him in the amateur Trans-Mississippi Tournament. I think Jack liked the effect that was created at The Golf Club.'' Dye then returned to Indianapolis and continued some unfinished work at Crooked Stick. ''Crooked Stick is built on a cornfield,'' he said, ''and I don't think there's a better golf course in the United States. In fact, when Toney Penna played Crooked Stick, he said he couldn't believe he was in Indiana. Again, I was very lucky. When I started Crooked Stick, I was on a MacKenzie kick, with a little bit of MacDonald thrown in. Then the people at Crooked Stick ran out of money for a while, and when I finally went back to finish the course, I was on my Ross and Tillinghast kicks. Somehow I got them all in there together, and to me Crooked Stick is as close to utopia as anyone may ever get.''

Later on in the 1960s, Nicklaus called Dye and asked if he'd like to build a course for Charles Frazier and the Sea Pines land development people down at Hilton Head Island. As it turned out, Frazier eventually commissioned Dye to create the Harbour Town links. Then Nicklaus got interested in the project and joined the operation as a consultant. ''It's funny how Harbour Town turned out,'' Dye said. ''Jack had input into the course, strong input. Another contributor was Charles Price, the golf writer who now lives at Hilton Head. I was working on the sixteenth hole and trying all kinds of things. Charlie came out and I said, 'Come up with an idea, Charlie, I've got to have something.' Well, Charlie walked around for a couple of hours, went back and got us a couple of beers, and then we talked for several hours about what the sixteenth hole ought to look like. I'm not ashamed to say it: the sixteenth hole was Charlie Price's idea. For that matter, the thirteenth green at Harbour Town belongs to my wife. Alice arrived one day when I was working on a drainage problem out at the eleventh hole, but she couldn't find me. She ran into one of my bulldozer operators at the thirteenth green, asked him what he was doing, and, well, she stayed there all day and, in effect, laid out the thirteenth green by having the bulldozer operator contour it the way she wanted. I got the drainage worked out there without making any major changes, then I brought her back out. 'Is this what you want?' I said. It was exactly what she wanted, so the thirteenth green at Harbour Town was designed by Mrs. Alice Dye, not Mr. Pete Dye.''

Dye stopped for a moment. ''I pride myself on the fact that I can take someone else's ideas,'' he said, ''and as long as they are consistent with what I'm trying to do . . . I can work them into my design for a championship-type course.''

Like all golf architects, Dye admittedly dreams of someday having the opportunity to build the utopia of golf courses, one layout in which he could bring together every strain of the distinct design philosophies. ''I'm afraid no one will ever get that chance,'' he said, ''because of the topographical and weather factors in various parts of the country, not to mention the state of the economy. For instance, maybe you'd want an oceanside hole with Bermuda grass and palm trees, and, well, if you were creating your utopia in, say, Buffalo, New York, you would not be able to have an oceanside hole with Bermuda grass and palm trees.'' Dye's theories on the ideal golf layout, though, provide an insightful look at what utopia might look like if a Dye ever gets the chance to create his dreams.

''Before I start,'' Dye said, ''let me make one thing clear: what really makes a golf course great is, first, the contouring around the greens and, second, the shape of the greens. You always hear people say that the size of a green should depend on the length of the shot normally played to the green; in other words, the longer the approach shot, the bigger the green. Not true. The size of a green is dictated by the severity of the hazards around that green and also by how the green itself is contoured. Here's a good example of what I mean, and of what I like to do. Call it deception. Donald Ross's first green at Pinehurst Number 2 is probably one hundred twenty feet long and fifty feet wide, and there is a severe bunker on the left side of the green. From the fairway, the green looks relatively flat; in fact, from front to back I

suspect that the difference in elevation is less than a foot. However, Ross created subtle contours in his greens, and the first green at Pinehurst Number 2 has more tricky little knolls than you can imagine. Anyway, standing in the fairway of the first hole, a good player will be looking at perhaps a seven-iron shot to the green. All that player really is thinking about, though, is that bunker to the left. 'Good Lord, I don't want to miss this shot to the left, not with that bunker there.'

''So, instead, faced with this mental uncertainty, he misses his shot to the right side, which looked wide open from back there in the fairway. Well, the right side *is* wide open, but Ross contoured it so severely that balls kick away and snuggle into teardrop grass mounds that guarantee anything but an even chip. To add to the golfer's sudden problems, the first green now is contoured *away* from him, and getting the ball close to the hole is a hazardous prospect. The architectural strategy of Mr. Ross was to make the golfer think he played a safe shot, then get to his ball and find that he put himself into a most difficult position.

''I'm the same way. I love to contour or bunker a green so severely to one side that golfers constantly fall into the trap of playing away from the obvious hazard only to end up in an even more precarious spot. Ernie Vossler, a strategic player when he was on the pro tour, once told me, 'Pete, I know when I'm playing one of your courses because when I miss a green on what appears to be the most hazardous side, I have a better shot for the pin than I would if I had missed the shot to the other side.' Of course, it's impossible to create this effect on all eighteen holes, but I try to do it as often as possible.

''On my utopia course,'' Dye continued, ''I'd definitely want to have four par-three holes, even though St. Andrews has only two par threes and some other great courses have as few as three par threes or as many as five. I also would want my par threes to be played in four different directions, with the longest par three played into the prevailing wind, and I'd want these holes spread throughout the golf course. The third and the seventh normally are good holes for par threes; so are the eleventh or twelfth and the sixteenth or seventeenth. Never the first hole, though, and never the eighteenth. I'd have a short par three of about one hundred and forty-five yards; a medium-short par three of about one hundred and sixty-five yards; a medium-long par three of about one hundred and eighty-five yards; and a long par three of about two hundred and twenty yards. My long and short par threes would be on one nine, the medium par threes on the other. On my short par three I'd insert very severe hazards, especially a deep bunker or two, totally or partially around the green. By deep

bunker, I mean one from which you cannot see the putting surface when you are standing in the sand. The green on this short par three could be as small as a postage stamp, with very subtle contours, or as large as the envelope, with severe contours, plateaus, and terraces. I constantly work on my par threes to make the shot from the tee and also the hazards very tricky.

"To me, the strength of a golf course rests in the par-four holes. I'd want ten or eleven of these par-four holes on my super course. Three or four of the par fours should be really long and hard, more than four hundred and thirty yards in length; three or four should be medium length, ranging from three hundred and ninety to four hundred and thirty yards; and three or four should be short par fours—like, oh, three hundred and thirty yards,

The first green at Donald Ross's Pinehurst Number 2 illustrates
a favorite Dye ploy—deception. The green, above, is spacious,
so that when the golfer on the fairway sees the deep trap
guarding the left side, opposite, he may push his approach
to the right, only to encounter a very tricky recovery, top.

three hundred and fifty-two, three hundred and sixty-five, three hundred and eighty-one. Really short by today's standards. In setting up my course, I'd place a short par four immediately before a long par four. Like my par threes, I'd like my short par fours to run in somewhat different directions, too, and they would be filled with hazards around the landing area off the tee and all around the green. What I'd really try to do, though, is to incorporate the subtleties of the natural topography into these short par fours. For instance, I'd attempt to create driving areas over streams or other major hazards, making the driving potential so severe that a good player,

Opposite: *Tree in a trap—a typical Dye innovation.* Above: *Water defines the South Course at John's Island, the eighth hole particularly.*

someone like a Jack Nicklaus, might feel that he should lay off his drive and hit a placement iron instead.

"Basically, on my ten or eleven par-four holes, I'd also have three or four holes with open landing areas for the tee shot, three or four with tight landing areas, and three or four with medium-size landing spots. Too many of today's architects, I'm afraid, subscribe to the double-jeopardy penal code and severely bunker *every* landing area. Listen, you can't have a four hundred and seventy-yard par four with several traps in the landing area. To me, balance is the key thing on these par-four holes. You also cannot have ten

four hundred and forty-yard par fours because four hundred and forty yards mean nothing to the Nicklauses and Millers and Palmers and all the kids who hit the ball half a mile. If every hole on a course is four-hundred and forty yards, the player who doesn't hit the ball out of sight gets beat to death. He has to hit a long iron approach to the green, while the maulers are cruising short irons to the flag. The architect must create par fours, using the terrain and the hazards to his best advantage, that won't definitely penalize the shorter hitter. So, on this utopia course, I'd have a couple of angle holes—I call dogleg holes 'angle' holes—from left to right, and a couple from right to left. I'd want to create as much diversification of shots as possible; I'd want the player to use all fourteen clubs in his bag.

"Finally, I'd have three or four par-five holes on my course. Most layouts now have at least four par fives, but I think you will see a lot of par seventy-one golf courses in the future, with only three par-five holes, eleven par fours and four par threes. On the whole it is difficult to find enough stretches of ideal ground to create four interesting par-five holes. If my utopia had four par fives, three of them would be gambling-type holes, where I'd try to entice the better golfers to blast away to the green on their second shot. These gambling par fives would not be much longer than a long par four, but the greens would be contoured and bunkered and protected in such a way that a poorly struck shot for the green would place the player in a hazardous location. My fourth par-five hole would be a monster, measuring at least six hundred yards—a hole that not even Nicklaus could reach in two with the wind at his back.

"To my way of thinking, the real trick to golf course architecture is to lure the golfer into a false sense of security. For instance, take the thirteenth hole at Augusta National, one of the great par fives in the world. Dr. MacKenzie created a left-side

hole, with wide-open space to the right. If you play your ball to the left and keep it there, then you can easily reach the green in two. If you play it to the right, though, you probably will not be able to carry the green with your second shot. Of course, the closer you play your ball to the left, the closer you are to all the hazards. So the risk is yours. Another simple illustration. On one of my par fives at Harbour Town, a player standing on the tee notices a long bunker on the left side—shallow but not too severe, with a flat bottom and a grassy face. The bunker looks a lot tougher than it really is. Meanwhile, to the right all the player sees is wide open space, so he aims his ball to the right side and, mindful of all the trouble on the left, winds up pushing the ball. Once he gets to his ball, he discovers that because of the bunkering and the trees in the vicinity of the green he is flat-out dead. There is no way he can hit the ball to the green. As the pros finally learned, the left side is the side to play if you want to make birdie on this par five, even though the most severe landing-area hazard is on that left side. My intention is to make the player take a chance.

"One word of caution, though. The worst thing an architect can do, I believe, is to set up the hazards on a hole so that he makes a guideline for the good player. If you place bunkers and trees on one side of a green, for example, and have water on the other side, the good player will guide the ball onto the putting surface, not hit it there."

Dye nodded his head. "That's my basic utopia," he said. Then he smiled. "Once you set down the layout, then the real work begins. I've always been an advocate of the old-course approach, where they planted different grasses to create different shots on each hole. Too many new courses in the United States have only one type of grass, for maintenance and cost reasons. On the old courses around the country and over in Great Britain, there are various types of grass on each hole. Fescue, velvet, bent, everything. As a result, three out of five times you may get a good lie in the rough, but the other two times you end up in the deep. The rub of the green. The greatest negotiator of golf shots in the world is Jack Nicklaus. Why? Because he was raised on Scioto, an old-style course, and has played in every imaginable competition in dozens of countries. He plays recovery shots as though they are second nature. On the other hand, a lot of these young kids on the tour, particularly the players who grew up on Bermuda grass, go into apoplexy when they are confronted with a shot from a clump of fescue. By using different

48

Above far left: *At the groundbreaking ceremony Dye, center, posed with Llywd Ecclestone, right, head of the John's Island corporate family.* Above left: *Carving out the jungle.* Left: *The course takes shape. The biggest problem was drainage; to keep the land dry, drainage ponds were used and connected to the river next to the property.*

Three of the more famous features of golf courses around the world—below: *the Church Pews of the third hole at Oakmont;* bottom: *the huge double green of the road hole at St. Andrews;* right: *the seventh green at Pebble Beach, a tiny target surrounded by sand and water.*

grasses, the architect can create one more shot
for the golfer to play.

"Look at it this way. The thing that an architect
must do is to create contrast and variety on his
golf course. Take this highway we're driving on
right now. The grass to the right of the road is one
color, and you can see the distinct line of the
roadway. Same with a golf course. The architect
ought to use whatever means he can to identify his
layout and define it. Never in my life did I think
that Harbour Town would be so well accepted by
the people who are supposedly experts on golf
courses. Well, what brought Harbour Town to life, I
think, was the contrast in the grasses. Until
Harbour Town, there had never been a course in
the Carolinas with different grasses. The contrast
in grasses has as much to do with the beauty of a
course as the bunkers, the water, the rough, the
trees."

Being from the old school of golf architecture, Dye
understandably loves sand traps. Unlike too many
architects, though, he does not use bunkers simply
for showcase reasons. "When I hear how some
new course has two hundred traps," Dye said, "I
really have to laugh. What good is a bunker if it is
not placed in a strategic position? Or if it is not
unique in style and design? For example, I use
bunkers with sand flashed up to the top, like most
architects, but I also use the Scottish-style
bunkers, with sand on the bottom but deep grass
on the very severe banks. And for my fairway
bunkers, particularly on the longer holes, I prefer
the wasteland effect—a long bunker with fairly
firm sand, from which the accomplished player
probably can play a good recovery. One of the
most thrilling recovery shots in golf, I think, is the
long bunker shot."

And what about the rough? "When cutting a
course," Dye said, "I like to leave as many trees as
possible on it because some day certain trees will
die due to the shock. At the same time I want the
maintenance people to control the trees and not

let them get too dense. What I want to create is a
rough from which a fantastic recovery shot is not
absolutely impossible. There always should be a
reward for the skill factor in golf. Indeed, if a
player misses one shot, he should have a chance
to hit his next shot back into play. Of course, I
don't think players should be able to smash drivers
out of the rough, but they should have the
opportunity to play some type of skillful recovery."

Dye smiled again. "I wonder what the course
record would be on my utopia layout?" he said.

In 1969, Mr. E. Llwyd Ecclestone, the man who
founded and developed the luxurious Lost Tree
Village complex in North Palm Beach, Florida,
purchased the three thousand acres that comprise
John's Island on the Atlantic Ocean, just north of
Vero Beach, Florida. John's Island is bordered by
two and a half miles of private ocean-front beach
on one side and by the Indian River and the

Intracoastal Waterway on the other. Ecclestone promptly undertook a ten-year plan to create a private residential resort community at John's Island. There were plans for private residences, ocean-front condominiums, golf cottages, townhouses, apartments, villas, a beach club, tennis courts, squash and racquetball courts, and, of course, not one but two "championship" golf courses. Six years into Ecclestone's ten-year plan, John's Island was already a thriving community, complete with all the facilities that Ecclestone and his associates had promised. Set in a perfectly splendid atmosphere, John's Island today ranks as one of the finest private residential resort communities in the world.

Pete Dye stood on the putting green behind the clubhouse at John's Island and shook his head. "When I first came here at Mr. Ecclestone's invitation," Dye said, "this part of John's Island—the golf courses, most of these

homes—was a swampy, wooded area with dense vegetation, rattlesnakes, coral snakes, alligators, and all the rest. Mr. Ecclestone told me that the management had to develop the area as quickly as possible and that he needed a golf course right away. I understood his problem."

Although Dye had never built an "instant" golf course, he immediately agreed to undertake the John's Island project. "I'm sure that Mr. Ecclestone thought I had a large staff and that I'd build his course from a complete set of engineering plans," Dye said. "Well, I don't work that way. I've never had a big staff. I have a few experienced people I always call on, but I prefer to use all local equipment and all local help. And I supervise the job personally. I'm not an absentee architect."

Dye began work on the South Course, the first course, at John's Island on April 1, 1970. "Mr. Ecclestone's people provided me with a survey of

the land," Dye said, "and then we were off on the job. I flew over the property in order to inspect the area, then I tramped through the swamp and the woods, carefully avoiding the snakes, to get a feel for the place." Dye, of course, had to keep the land developers in mind, for they really had first call on the land for the residences. Dye will not discuss the subject, but if he had had first right of refusal on the John's Island property, the South Course no doubt would have been laid out partly along the ocean, not completely inland.

"The first thing I did," Dye said, "was make a routing of the course, a routing, incidentally, that I changed probably fifty times before the course was completed. For the most part, routing is a simple matter on a Florida piece of land because the architect does not have to fight the unique but natural par-three hole. Like at Jack Nicklaus's new Memorial Course at Muirfield Village in Columbus, Ohio, where the topography led to the construction of some natural par threes. There are no ravines,

for instance, to worry about in Florida. At John's Island, the real trick was to get the holes to run primarily north and south, with the general flow of the land. By doing this, we also provided the developers with the best possible parcels of property for residential use. They wanted the golf course on both sides of most of the houses, and in the end we managed to work it out that way. On the South Course, the residents now have either golf course or water frontage, or both."

In routing the course, Dye measured the lengths and widths on the survey, laid out his eighteen holes, then showed the design to the developers. "It's a game of numbers, in a way," Dye said. "You know inherently that you want landing areas that are fifty yards wide and that you'd like to have a total of fifty yards of rough alongside the fairway. Then you put in a road and a house on both sides —another one hundred and twenty-five, one hundred and fifty yards or so—and add it all up. When I went back to Mr. Ecclestone and his

Samples of Dye's par threes show a distinct similarity.
Above: *The thirteenth at John's Island.* Opposite top: *Sixth green at Crooked Stick.* Opposite bottom left *and* right: *Seventh hole and fourteenth green at Harbour Town Links.*

54

people, they said that on some holes I didn't give them enough room to develop a road with houses on both sides, and on other holes I gave them too much room. So I kept going back to the routing board until we got everything squared away.''

Dye's initial routing pattern for the eighteen holes on the South Course at John's Island showed only three things: prospective tees, landing areas, and greens, all of which could be changed to accommodate the topographical problems Dye might encounter at the site. ''I gave my son, Perry, the routing survey,'' Dye said, ''and, per custom, told him to take his men out and cut a trunk line, a three-foot-wide swath, up and down the course that would show where the holes would go. Perry and the engineers cleared their narrow path down my first hole, but as they were doing the second hole, Perry suddenly told them to stop, that it didn't look right. Sure enough, the slide rules had gone wacky. Instead of going south for the second hole, they were now going west. How Perry knew something was wrong, I'll never know. Instinct, I guess.''

When Perry and the engineers had completed their job, Dye returned to John's Island and began to stake the course with the help of his other son, Petey. He tramped through the swamp again to determine where the greens should be, then marked them accordingly. ''John's Island was practically under water, remember, so we had to find high areas for the greens,'' Dye said. ''As it turned out, solving the drainage problem was the toughest part of our job at John's Island. The water table was only a few feet below the surface, and we had to drain it slowly in order to keep the trees alive and dry the land properly. We had no alternative. If we had built up the marshland by filling it in, we would have killed all the trees. You cannot save trees by piling dirt around them.''

In working out the drainage problems at John's Island, Dye also had to conform to the rules of Florida's ecology department. ''What the ecology

Overleaf: *Impressive though it was, the finished product was not quite as planned. After Dye had finished, his front and back nines were switched, creating a certain imbalance. To appreciate the diversity Dye built into his course,* compare the short, intricate thirteenth, *top,* and sixteenth, *opposite,* to the long, spacious fifteenth, *above.*

people wanted, and rightfully so," Dye said, "was for the water to flood the golf course, not the residences, during any hurricanes or other major storms. So we had to lay out the course and organize the drainage so that the fairways were built below the level of the lots surrounding them. At John's Island the greens are all elevated between six and seven feet above sea level and also above the basic level of the fairways. The adjacent Indian River is exactly at sea level. To keep the land dry, we put in some drainage ponds and connected them to the river, and we also set up the fairway drains so that they, too, go back into the river. At the same time, we sized the fairway drains so that we can regulate the speed at which the water enters the river. It's all very scientific." He laughed. "My education background in the drainage department, incidentally, is zero.

"When we were ready to attack the holes, I gave the bulldozer operators very specific instructions. I told them to start three hundred feet in front of the tees I had staked out and clear a one hundred-foot swath down the middle of the holes to within two hundred feet of the green positions I had staked, then push everything into the middle and burn it. They did this for all eighteen holes. When they finished the eighteenth hole, the smoldering at the first hole had stopped. They had cleared only about eight hundred of the twelve hundred or so feet on the average hole, and now it was time for me to do my thing."

As always, Dye did his thing with a basket of ribbons. "I like to play with each hole in order to acquire a certain instinctive feel for the golf shot or shots that will have to be played on that hole," he said. So, standing on, say, the first tee, Dye visualized the type of drive that would have to be played into the landing area. "I went down both sides of the fairway and put ribbons on the trees that I wanted to remain on the layout," he said. "Then I went back to the tee again and tried to

visualize the shot one more time. If I didn't like what I saw, I went back out and changed the ribbons around. I changed them as many times as I felt necessary. I had to get my feel for the hole. Then I did the same thing up around the green, marking the trees I wanted to keep on the final layout." He stopped. "Some people think that my approach is too time consuming. Listen: If I had the bulldozers clear the whole hole, I might find myself walking down and saying, 'Gee, it sure would be nice to have a tree here, so let's plant one.' By doing it my way, I don't have to plant any trees where I just knocked some down." Once Dye finished his ribbon job on a hole, he sent his men back out to remove the rest of the trees and other debris from the layout. "Sometimes we had to do this by hand," he said, "but it was worth it."

By the time Dye finished the ribbon part of the project and the remaining trees and brush had been cut down, he believed that the South Course had the feel of a superb layout. "It opened with three good holes, demanding but not severely penal; moved into a stretch of four extremely difficult holes; then gave the golfer a breather on the eighth and ninth holes. The back nine started with a very tough par four, eased off just a bit for a couple of holes, then closed with five excellent tests of golf. I was very pleased with the layout."

For his final acts before seeding the course, Dye contoured the fairways, inserting bunkers and building some mounds, and shaped the greens as well as the areas around the green, placing bunkers here, tricky little mounds there, and subtle knolls, nicks, bumps, clumps, and depressions everywhere. Dye is a fan of railroad ties, perhaps because they are found all over the great old courses in Scotland, and he used them to wall some bunkers and some greens and, at the same time, to prevent natural erosion of the land. He also is very particular about his greens. "I get a vision about my greens, about how I want them to look," he said. "I start off by having the bulldozer man shape the greens the way I want them. Then, when he gets finished, we go back out together and redo the greens four, five, ten times if necessary. I play at least a full day with each green until I get the feel I want. I guess I spend, oh, about eight thousand dollars rechanging the greens—dropping the surface an inch here, raising it an inch there, widening it, narrowing it—but what's eight thousand dollars on a seven hundred and fifty thousand-dollar project?''

Unlike most architects, Dye will not seed a golf course until he has completely finished with the contouring and the shaping of all the holes and all the greens. ''The owners want you to plant as soon as you finish each hole,'' he said, ''but I stall them. Who knows? Maybe I'll change the eighth green at the very last second.'' For the South Course, Dye planted a strain of hybrid Bermuda grass called Tif-dwarf just before Labor Day in 1970. Three months later, on December 1, the South Course was opened for play. ''All told, we gave them their instant course in less than eight months,'' Dye said. ''They were pretty happy with it, too.''

In the end, unknown to Dye, the developers made a major change in his layout for the course: they reversed the nines and started the South Course with Dye's tenth hole, not his first. ''For traffic-control reasons,'' someone explained to Dye. Whatever the reason or reasons, by switching the nines the developers somewhat ruined the flow that he, like all architects, tries to build into a golf course. For instance, the first hole at John's Island, or Dye's tenth, now is a treacherous 421-yard dogleg-left par four, with a severe driving area and a very shallow green, fronted by a difficult bunker. A killing hole, to say the least, and one that no great architect would ever use to start a course. Although Dye keeps silent on the subject, he obviously does not appreciate what the developers did to his grand design. ''It's their golf course now,'' he said. The utopian golf course, it would seem, remains in Pete Dye's mind.

The South Course was only the first of two Dye courses at John's Island. The finishing hole on the North Course, this par five begins amid the same sort of water channels that permeate the South Course, but on the whole the North Course is distinctly different.

2
Sweet Spots and Sore Spots
The Equipment Jungle

It's the middle of February. You have just collected your bonus check for exceeding the company's sales quota for the previous year, and, well, you think you need a new set of golf clubs more than your golf widow needs a new cloth coat or the kitchen a new refrigerator. So you drop in on your friendly pro, who is sporting a deep tan after spending the required four months in Florida, and say, "Gee, Fred, I'd like to buy a new set of clubs."

"Sure, pards," says Fred. "What can we get for you? Cast or forged heads? Graphites, titaniums, borons, or just plain old steel shafts? And how do you want the shafts? Stiff, flex, firm, medium, or soft? We've got some new pro-pel shafts if you'd like to try them, too. What about the swing weight? D-1, D-2, D-3, D-4, or D-5—or maybe as light as C-9? What about the length? Standard? Half an inch short? An inch short? Half an inch long? An inch long? And the grips? Standard size, or do you want them built up—a thirty-second of an inch? A sixteenth? Rubber or leather? (We have them both.) Where do you want the weight on the irons —in the hosel or in the head? For the woods, do you want epoxy, glass, or aluminum inserts? What color heads? How much loft in the face of the driver? Do you want the faces open or hooked? And while you're at it, we have a big sale on golf balls. How many dimples do you want? Would you like ninety compression or a hundred? More or less drag? Pro-traj or regular traj? What's your preference for initial velocity? Oh yes, we have a choice of covers for the golf balls, too, and if you'd like your name on them, we can handle that."

Befuddled now, you try to salvage some of your composure by making a decision. "Ahhh, yeah, sure, Fred. Put my name on the golf balls so I won't lose them."

Listen, this is not a laughing matter, not when a new set of clubs—three woods (a driver, a three-wood, and either a four-wood or a five-wood) and ten irons (two-iron through nine-iron, plus a pitching wedge and a sand wedge)—costs about $2,250 for graphite shafts, $1,750 for titanium shafts, and as much as $700 for regular old steel shafts. You would like to think you are spending that kind of money for a worthy cause, your game. So to start, here is a crash course in the anatomy of a golf club, after which you should be able at least to understand the questions in the arcane procedure of selecting golf clubs, if not yet have quite all the answers.

The Shafts

Graphite and titanium are just the latest of the "revolutionary new" shafts produced for golf clubs. First the old hickory shaft gave way to steel. Then fiberglass was introduced, though not with great success, followed by aluminum, which bombed. Aluminum proved to be too soft for golf club shafts. The clubhead of an aluminum-shafted club would strike the ball not with a crisp click but a dull thud, and more often than not the ball wouldn't go very far. Stainless steel came next, and finally, graphite and titanium, both of which can be highly effective but are very expensive.

The Shakespeare Golf Company, which had worked long and hard on fiberglass shafts, gets much of the credit for the introduction of graphite shafts. In 1968, Shakespeare initiated a research project to find a shaft that would be superior to stainless steel. The new shaft would have to be light in weight, very strong, and even stiffer than steel. Shakespeare rejected a number of materials, then settled on Union Carbide's new Thornel® graphite fibers. According to Shakespeare,

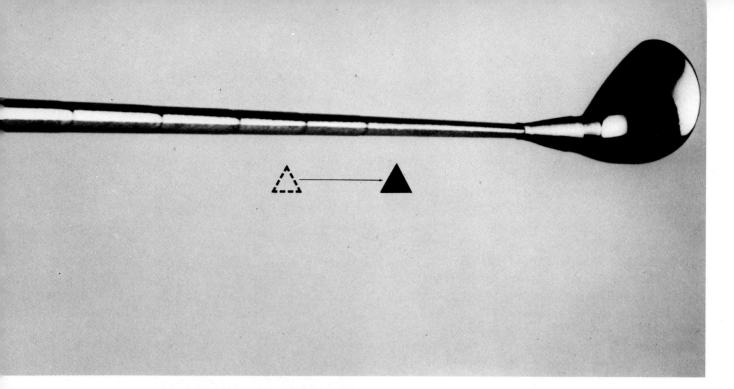

Above: *Lighter than steel—the essence of the great graphite advance. Because they are lighter, the graphite-shafted clubs have a lower center of gravity and, thus, are whippier and potentially more powerful.* Left: *Frank Thomas, later to become the United States Golf Association's certified equipment maven, helped develop the graphite-shafted club.*

The graphite club is made by wrapping the graphite fibers in alignment with the stresses a swing imparts to the club.

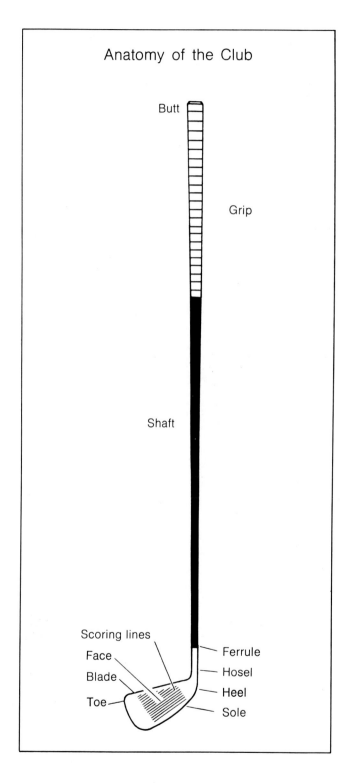

Anatomy of the Club

Butt

Grip

Shaft

Scoring lines

Face

Blade

Toe

Ferrule

Hosel

Heel

Sole

Thornel® graphite consists 99 percent of carbon atoms linked in such a fashion that in fiber form the material is approximately three times stronger than steel in tension and four times lighter.

To make this Thornel® fiber into a golf shaft, more than 900,000 fibers are impregnated with a high-performance epoxy resin and placed in predetermined directions on a mandrel. The epoxy is cured and the mandrel removed, thus forming the hollow shaft.

The catch to these new, lighter-shafted clubs is that they must be swung more slowly than the heavier, steel-shafted clubs. Because they are lighter only in the shaft, they are whippier, with a greater proportion of their weight concentrated in the hosel and clubhead. If you swing them with the same force as steel-shafted clubs, your hands will move through the first half of the swing too fast, out of sync with the clubhead. However, if you do slow your swing, you can still generate greater clubhead speed than you would with steel-shafted clubs, and hence greater distance on your shots.

The Shakespeare Company attributes the popularity of the new kind of shaft to precisely this advance: You do less work for more gain. However, because graphite is so expensive, the trend to it has not been overwhelming. Most golfers who do use graphite have only one such club—the driver. The other clubs don't seem to be worth the extra expense. One amateur golfer explained, "I didn't mind paying a hundred fifty dollars for a graphite-shafted driver because I hit the driver about fourteen times each round. But I wasn't about to spend that kind of money for, oh, a two-iron, which I hit maybe once every other round."

Some companies have made scientific refinements and improvements in their graphite shafts. Aldila, another of the firms that helped pioneer the production of the graphite shaft, now adds boron to its graphite shafts. Boron, Aldila claims, is twice as strong but only one-third the weight of steel and 25 percent stronger than graphite. Aldila contends that its shaft with boron is 15 percent, or one-half ounce, lighter than any other graphite shaft. Johnny Miller used Aldila's boron-graphite shafts when he won the 1976 British Open Championship and reportedly remarked afterward, ''They are so good that it's like cheating.''

Like graphite, titanium is very light. A titanium shaft is about 44 percent lighter than a steel one. And, like graphite, titanium shafts, when used properly—that is, swung slowly—will drive the ball farther than steel.

This principle of revamped weight distribution that lies behind the lighter-shafted clubs has been adapted to steel in pro-pel shafts, which have greater tensile strength and weight near the bottom of the shaft. Thus, the pro-pel club is whippier, with the potential for shooting the ball higher more quickly than other steel clubs, which are stronger near the grip.

This is a good moment to explain swing weight, which is the overall balance of the club, determined by its weight and the distribution of the weight through the club. It is calculated by a mathematical formula known as the ounce-inch ratio. If you have trouble balancing your checkbook, or even if you don't, don't worry about the ounce-inch ratio. You need only know that it is converted into readings such as D-2 and C-9, and the higher the reading, the heavier the club feels to the golfer as he swings it. Letters closer to the start of the alphabet are considered lower readings, so, for example, C-9 is lighter than D-2.

Sweet Spots

The sweet spot of a golf clubhead is the percussion center—the point at which the clubhead will not vibrate when it strikes the ball, and hence the point through which force can be delivered most efficiently. In short, hit a ball on the clubhead's sweet spot and the ball will go farther.

Some time ago one manufacturer came up with the idea of an expanded sweet spot and had some success with it in the marketplace. All the others adopted the rhetoric, and claims of expanded sweet spots became a hot item in the trendy world of golf huckstering. They are, if not a total fraud, at least an obfuscation of the facts.

The location of the sweet spot is determined by where the shaft meets the clubhead, and since the United States Golf Association has decreed that the shaft must join the clubhead at its neck or heel, the sweet spot can't move. It's always about an inch away from the shaft. Nor can it be expanded. The best the clubmakers have been able to do is to put more weight in the clubhead, allowing for the possibility of a stronger sweet spot. Some have even slipped lead weights behind the clubface.

Here is a claim from a typical advertisement:
Brand X—18.3% of the total iron-head weight is in the hosel. Hosel weight that in no way contributes to the playability of the iron. Example: Hosel Weight—45 grams. Power Area Weight—201 grams. Total Iron Weight—246 grams.
Our Iron—only 8.1% of the total iron-head weight remains in the hosel. Approximately one extra ounce is added to the important power area through our patented process, yet total weight remains the same. Example: Hosel Weight—20 grams. Power Area Weight—226 grams. Total Iron Head Weight—246 grams.

Also, manufacturers have dispersed the weight on the clubhead, allowing for stronger shots that are struck with the clubface's heel, toe, and base, not parts of the sweet spot. Still others have produced clubs with movable weights, supposedly allowing a player to create his own sweet spot by adjusting the weight cartridges. As a result, some golf clubheads have grown to be almost as big as snow shovels. They are a lot less reliable than the smaller clubheads, and at least one pro denies that there is more power in them. He says, "The bigger the clubhead, the less chance you have of hitting the exact type of shot you want. And the bigger the clubhead, the shorter distance you will hit the ball."

In any case, you can forget about expanded sweet spots.

Length of Clubs

Just because you happen to be 6 feet 4 inches tall doesn't necessarily mean you need clubs longer than the standard length. Tom Weiskopf, who stands 6 feet 3 inches, uses clubs that are actually one-half inch shorter than the standard length. In fact, Weiskopf's clubs are shorter than the clubs used by Jack Nicklaus, even though Weiskopf is four inches taller than Nicklaus. Why? Because the proper criterion for determining the length of your clubs is not your height but the relative position of your arms to the ground when you let them hang naturally at your sides. When Weiskopf drops his arms to his sides, his fingertips almost reach his knees. On the other hand, when Nicklaus drops his arms to his sides, his fingertips rest well above the knee. Nicklaus's fingertips are higher from the ground than are Weiskopf's, so Nicklaus needs clubs slightly longer than Weiskopf's. Take note: Two different individuals can be 5 feet 1 inch or 6 feet 6 inches and still need the same length clubs. Check according to your fingertips.

Degree of Loft

Degree of loft is the angle the clubface makes with the perpendicular of the ground. The greater the angle, the greater the degree of loft in the club and in the shot it produces. As everyone knows, clubs are most commonly classified by their degree of loft, from number-one woods (least loft) to sand wedges (most loft). However, not all clubs of a like classification have the same degree of loft. A one-wood's loft, for example, may be as great as 12 or as small as 9. Stronger swingers

need less loft in their clubs, weaker swingers more, but the room for variation is minimal because, as you'll see by checking the chart below, the standard difference in loft between one club and the next one in line is not very great.

Standard Degrees of Loft and Standard Lengths for a Set of Golf Clubs

CLUB	DEGREE OF LOFT	MEN'S	WOMEN'S
one-wood	11	43 inches	42 inches
two-wood	13	42½ inches	41½ inches

The manufacturer of this club claims that it has not an expanded sweet spot but a "sweetened" one, i.e., a more powerful one, because of the lead weight behind it (arrow).

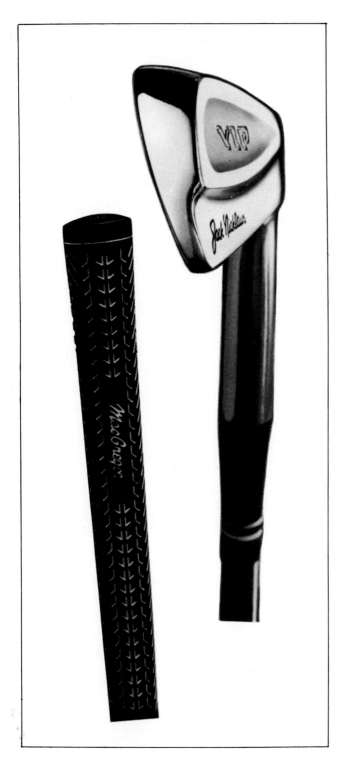

three-wood	16	42 inches	41 inches
four-wood	19	41½ inches	40½ inches
five-wood	21	41 inches	40 inches
one-iron	17	39 inches	38 inches
two-iron	20	38½ inches	37½ inches
three-iron	23	38 inches	37 inches
four-iron	27	37½ inches	36½ inches
five-iron	31	37 inches	36 inches
six-iron	35	36½ inches	35½ inches
seven-iron	39	36 inches	35 inches
eight-iron	43	35½ inches	34½ inches
nine-iron	47	35 inches	34 inches
pitching wedge	51	35 inches	34 inches
sand wedge	56	35 inches	34 inches

If you've understood most or all of this, don't get overconfident. The fact that you understand some of the lingo doesn't mean you know enough to decide which brand to buy. Consider, for a moment, the scene at a recent annual merchandise show staged by the Professional Golfers' Association (PGA) at the new Disney World complex in Lake Buena Vista, Florida. This was no Mickey Mouse production. Some 84 manufacturers displayed more than 1,000 model

Those autographed models you buy at the pro shop bear little resemblance to the clubs the pros use, which is just as well since the pros require different clubs than everyone else. For example, they can handle much stiffer shafts.

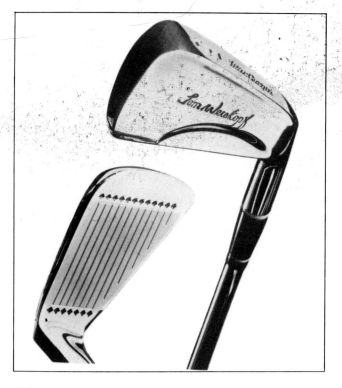 

lines of golf clubs and putters. (For the record, another 32 companies displayed hundreds of styles of golf bags, one of which featured a pull-down seat and a pull-out flask. Some 26 firms exhibited more than 400 types of golf balls, including creations called "the Stinger" and "the Attack." There were golf balls for rain, for snow, for sun, and honest, even a golf ball with a self-contained beeping device. "When you hit our ball into the rough," chirped a publicist, "just follow the sound of the beep and you'll always find it." Asked what happens when a beeper ball is hit into the water, the publicist reflected, "I don't know. I play tennis myself. I guess the beeper drowns.")

Can anyone make sense of all this promotional overkill? Who knows? Not even the touring pros can agree on which clubs are best. Most pros carry several different makes, this despite their affiliation with only one particular club

manufacturer. Nor can one find anything approaching consensus among the club professionals, the people who sell most of the golf equipment in the country. At a recent PGA national club professionals' championship in Georgia, the 353 players used 31 different makes of woods, 29 different makes of irons, and 10 different makes of golf balls. Moreover, more often than not these pros preferred mixed sets of woods to the sets of any one manufacturer.

To complicate matters a bit further, most of the leading touring professionals switch club makes and models and change their golf ball brands when they compete in a tournament abroad. The reason: they all hold lucrative endorsement contracts with foreign manufacturers, not to mention equally profitable clothing endorsement contracts. Of course, in most cases those foreign-made clubs and balls are almost perfect duplicates of the clubs and balls the players use at

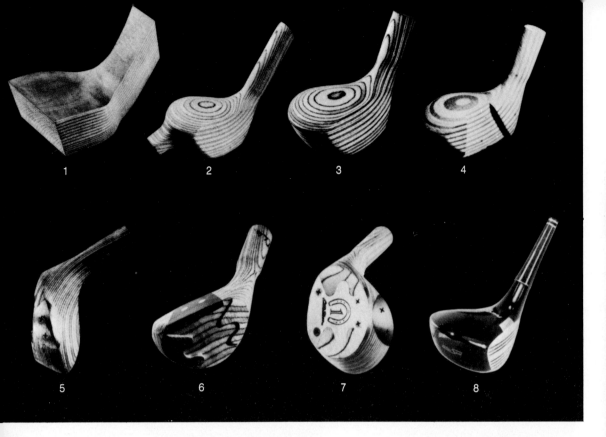

Above: *A wood block becomes a wood head: the blank is shaped to the manufacturer's specifications (2); the "nose" that held the head in the profiling machine is cut off (3); cutout is made for face insert (4); brass back is added (5); face insert is bonded in place (6); sole plate is attached (7); and face is scored after varnishing (8). Opposite: Fastening the brass back (step 5).*

home. The greatest change is in the brand name.

And now the crusher. Even if you could decide that some pro had discovered the perfect set of clubs, you probably couldn't buy them anyway. In fact, those autograph models for sale in pro shops and in sporting goods stores are about as similar to the clubs the autographing pro uses as a Vespa motor scooter is to a Mercedes. "I don't know of any pro who plays the same clubs as the public buys, no matter what the signature on the clubs," says Jack Nicklaus.

How then to choose a brand? Perhaps the experience of Nicklaus himself is most instructive. In 1976, for the Bing Crosby tournament, Nicklaus began using a new set of irons, a set that was to be the prototype for a new design that the manufacturer, MacGregor, would eventually make available to the public. Nicklaus had used his old set of irons from April 1967 (starting the week after he had missed the cut at Augusta as the defending champion in the Masters Tournament) through the Australian PGA Championship of 1975, a tournament he won by a wide margin. However, after nine years of constant use by the greatest player ever to strike a ball, those clubs were worn out. Nicklaus had had the grooves on the irons filed down so often that the faces of the irons looked almost sheer.

Nicklaus had designed the model of the new clubs himself, with some help from David Graham, an Australian touring pro who is associated with Nicklaus in a club-making venture. For 63 holes of the Crosby tournament, Jack's new clubs seemed to work perfectly. He led the tournament with nine holes to play, and when the television commentators picked up play at Pebble Beach on Sunday, all they talked about was Nicklaus's superb new clubs. On the par-four thirteenth hole, Nicklaus drove the ball perfectly and had just a six-iron shot to the green left. As he stood over the shot, Nicklaus was slightly below the ball, since the fairway sloped down from the right to the left.

Then it happened. He made a terrible swing, turning at the top and almost casting the club, as a fisherman might a fly rod. He hooked the shot, and the ball ended up far left of the green, hole-high but perhaps forty yards from the pin.

Suddenly, the television commentators decided that the new clubs weren't so wonderful after all. There had to be something wrong with them, the announcers reasoned, because Nicklaus never hits such bad shots. Then, when Nicklaus scuffed his approach shot and the ball rolled back to him, the announcers informed the American public that Jack's new clubs obviously were not fit for competition.

In fact there was very little wrong with the six-iron, or any of the other clubs. Nicklaus had simply hit the type of golf shot that all those amateurs who use Jack Nicklaus autograph clubs hit all the time. For the rest of the round, Nicklaus hit more bad golf shots than he had in about five years. He had not played competitive golf in almost two months, and as he admitted later, his swing simply deserted him. For the last nine holes of the Crosby, Nicklaus shot a disastrous 45—nine over par, or a bogey a hole—and for the round he slumped to 82.

Later, Nicklaus suggested that he probably should not have played with the new irons, but at the same time he accepted fully the blame for the disastrous finish. "The grooves were too deep," he said. "I found that I was hitting my six-iron, say, only as far as I normally hit a seven-iron, and because of the too-deep recesses in the face, the ball had too much spin and backed up too much. I was able to compensate for that easily enough, but I was never able to compensate for the terrible swings I made those last several holes."

So the clubs went back to the factory, and Nicklaus visited the swing doctor. A few weeks later, with another set of irons and his swing restored, Nicklaus won the prestigious PGA Tournament Players Division (TPD) championship.

MacGregor began to market the new Nicklaus-designed clubs shortly thereafter.

The moral? As the gun lovers might say, golf clubs don't make golf shots; people do. It may well be that the wisest thing you can do with that bonus check is go back to Fred, the friendly pro, tell him you've decided to send out your old clubs to be refinished, and use the rest of the money for a new refrigerator after all.

With that cynical recommendation in mind, let's attempt to quell two more particularly virulent strains of equipment hysteria—those occasioned by putters and by balls. As documented more fully later in this book, it takes a golfer with serene confidence in his putting—sometimes almost a contradiction in terms, it seems—to resist the latest craze over putters. So it is perhaps not surprising to find relatively little fickleness among the touring pros, who have for the most part learned to cope with, if not master, the aggravating task of putting. For almost all his career, Nicklaus has used a George Low-model flange. Arnold Palmer, whose putting has grown increasingly unreliable as he has aged—some say he has developed the Ben Hogan "yips"—alternates putters frequently now, but tends to stay with variations of the flange model. (In the basement club repair and storage room of his office building, adjacent to his home in Latrobe, Pennsylvania, Palmer has stored perhaps one thousand putters, and during the course of a season he tries a majority of them on the putting green across the road at the Latrobe Golf Club, which he owns.) Johnny Miller has used the same Bull's Eye putter since his days at Brigham Young. Lee Trevino has been a flange man since the days when he was hustling for nickels around Dallas.

Still, among the touring pros there is a faction as impressionable as any amateur about the newest putter sensation. Several years ago, an inventive manufacturer produced a putter called "the Potato Masher," and it was a popular putter among some fringe players for about six months. When its appeal faded, one pro who had bought the club gave it to his wife for a Christmas present, only to be informed by her that she had never mashed a potato in her life and didn't intend to start. The Potato Masher became a donation to charity.

The standard rule for selecting a putter is: heavy for slow greens, light for fast greens. But this dictum applies only to golfers who play the same course most of the time. Most of the pros prefer to use flange-style putters that are halfway between light blades and heavy mallets, because the texture and quality of the greens they play vary from week to week. In one tournament they may play on slow, Bermuda greens, in the next on fast, bent grass greens. Rather than switch putters each week and continually try to get accustomed to a new feel, they compromise and choose one putter they can use comfortably on both fast and slow surfaces.

In recent years most putter manufacturers have tried to create a blade in which the whole face comprises a sweet spot. With many of these putters, you can get the same roll and distance from a putt stubbed on the toe as you can with a putt hit squarely in the center of the blade. Of course, most good putters prefer a putter with a particular sweet spot, preferably closer to the heel than the toe, in part because they like to use the other, less lively parts of the putter blade to control the shorter, more delicate putts they face each round. Good putters invariably handle short, twisting, downhill putts by striking the ball on the toe of the putter. This deadens the putt and makes it easier to control.

The latest innovation in putters is a model called "the Zebra," which costs $55—more than double the price of the average putter—and just may be an improvement on it. Like other modern putters, the Zebra features a sweet spot that comprises the entire blade. In addition, the shaft of the Zebra

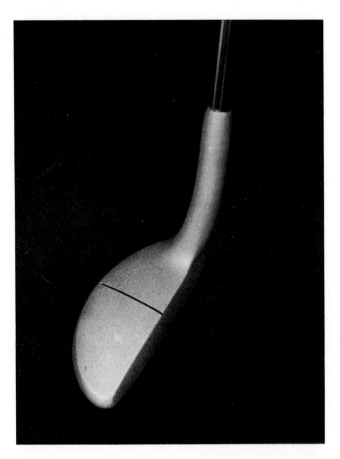

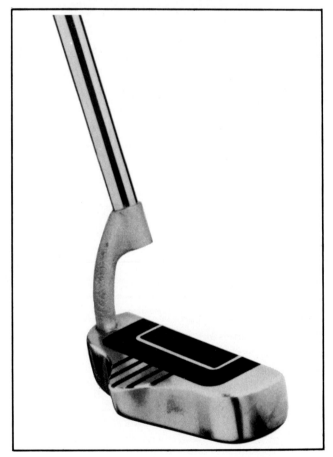

As if putting were not strain enough, one must select a putter from a seemingly limitless range of alternatives. Gimmickry is flourishing. That mitteny thing on the far right, for example, is simply the garbed version of the Zebra putter adjacent to it.

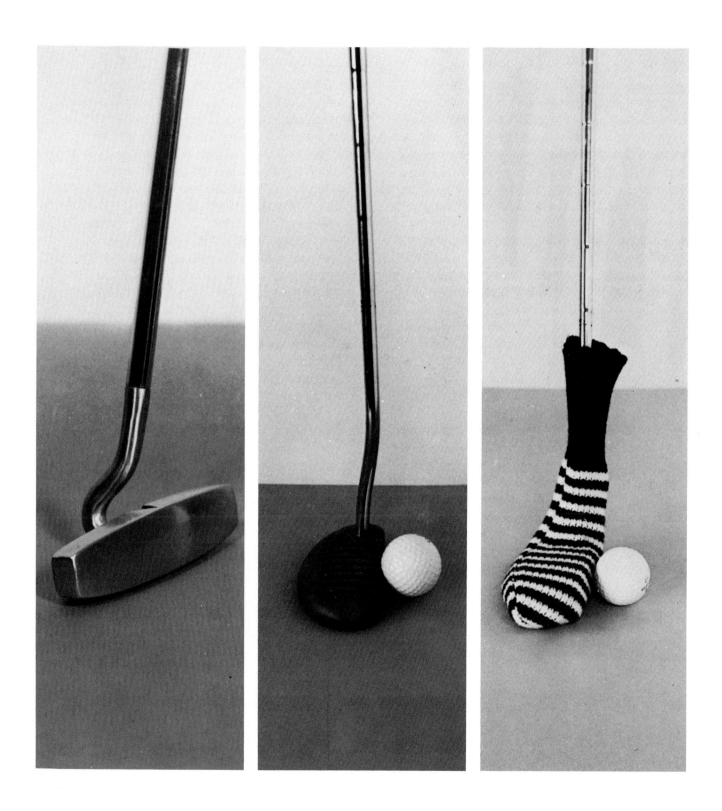

attaches to the head about one-fourth of the way from the heel, and the shaft is slightly offset in such a way that the golfer's hands at address are positioned in front of the ball, which is exactly the position the instructional books recommend. And by removing a plate on the bottom of the head, you can add or subtract weights to make the club heavier or lighter, thus adjusting it to the speed of the greens on which you are putting. (The USGA prohibits a golfer from tampering with his putter during a round, however.) The most enticing feature of the Zebra is its black and gray stripes, 11 in all, on its low, half-moon, mallet-style head. You line up your ball against the edges of the stripes and then strike the ball along that line. "The Zebra stripes definitely help you line your putt up squarely," testifies one pro, "and they really force you to bring the putter back and through on a straight line."

The Zebra first came on the market in 1975 and sold like crazy immediately. Sales got a boost in the spring of 1976 when Raymond Floyd used a Zebra in winning the Masters. Zebra stripes on a putter became the height of style. "The thing I like best about the Zebra putter," laughed one fashion-conscious golfer, "is not the putter itself but the knitted black and white striped Zebra cover that comes with it. It's a great conversation piece. I don't know a good putter from a bad putter, but when people ask me what's under that Zebra cover, I put on my airs, and well, you'd think I had just won the U.S. Open. It's all part of the act, isn't it?"

No technological advance in equipment is so substantial, it would appear, that it can resist a little gimmickry to enhance it. If the future holds a psychedelic-colored mallet, in the contemplation of which the golfer standing over a putt will achieve a trancelike serenity that will banish all distracting or upsetting thoughts, one can confidently expect that this magic wand will come with suitably spaced-out extras—a cover exuding

a mildly hallucinogenic scent and sporting a design to induce vertigo.

It is the job of the USGA to decide which of these innovations are legitimate improvements, or at worst harmless peculiarities, and which threaten the integrity of the game. As Technical Director of the USGA, Frank Thomas is very involved with this validation process. He is a research scientist who tests golf clubs and golf balls to make certain that they conform to the specifications of the two ruling bodies of the sport, the USGA and the Royal and Ancient Golf Society of St. Andrews. Thomas's small office at USGA headquarters, in Far Hills, New Jersey, is cluttered with countless inventors' creative fruits, most of them unacceptable to the USGA. Among other clubs sent to Thomas for inspection during a recent period were a putter with mirrors attached to it (to help the player line up his putt), and a driver with a grip molded to fit each individual player's hands so that they automatically fell into perfect grip position. As usual, Thomas returned both pieces of equipment to their inventors with a simple note explaining that the clubs did not conform to USGA specifications and, as such, could not be used in USGA-sanctioned competition.

"My job," says Thomas, "is to protect the game of golf—to protect it for the golfer, the manufacturer, and the game itself. Golf is one game where we attempt to maintain traditions. After all, golf has been one challenging game since 400 A.D. or so, and to last that length of time, there must be something we've done right."

In testing, Thomas never draws formal conclusions that might document the claim of one manufacturer against another. "It's safe to say," he says, "that nobody knows exactly what kind of equipment is best for one particular individual. Golf is about eighty percent psychological. It is a matter of how you think at certain times. All we do here at the USGA is set up performance standards that clubs and balls must meet, and certainly not exceed. We know that manufacturers are capable of producing weapons—clubs and balls—that could turn even the most difficult five hundred fifty-yard par five into a simple little seven-iron shot, but then the game wouldn't be golf anymore. Our job is to protect the game from that sort of thing.''

The list of the USGA's standards and specifications is a formidable one. Clubs must not exceed a certain length, and the shafts and the clubfaces must remain within certain dimensions. Thomas adds, ''We are very concerned as to where the shaft of a club enters the head. To be a golf club, the shaft must enter at the end, at the heel. If it enters in the middle, it is not a golf club anymore.''

In general, Thomas and the USGA tend to look favorably on improvements that demand an undiminished degree of skill from the golfer, no matter how much they can help him. The organization approved graphite- and titanium-shafted clubs, for example, because they benefit only a golfer who can compensate for the lightness of the clubs by swinging slower than he would with steel shafts.

Thomas does some of his most interesting work with golf balls, which he checks for such things as initial velocity, dimple count, dimple configuration, weight, and size. Each year he rejects dozens of new balls forwarded for his approval.

Dimples, of course, decrease the drag of a ball and thereby help the lift. If you strike a smooth, undimpled golf ball with, say, your driver, you probably would not hit it more than a hundred yards. However, with the same swing at a dimpled golf ball, you'd probably produce a shot of some two hundred twenty yards. Some ball manufacturers have introduced balls with hexagonal dimples, claiming that the ball will bore through the air more easily and travel a greater distance. One company has introduced a ball with deeper, smaller dimples than its regular ball,

A matter of dimples. In 1973, Acushnet altered the exterior of its Titleist ball. Look closely at the two balls above, and you'll discover that the one on the right, the new model, has larger, shallower dimples. Moreover, the new model, left, has a more uniform configuration of dimples than the old one, below left.

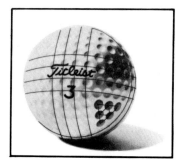

claiming that the ball flies lower but farther. "Don't think the golfing public isn't aware of all these claims," says one club pro. "I love it when a twenty-four-handicap player walks into the shop and says he needs a ball with plenty of square dimples. He's probably not going to get the ball into the air no matter what he hits, but he has bought the program from all the advertisements."

As for other aspects of the golf ball cover, the manufacturers have produced a definite dollar-saving for most amateurs in the ball covering Surlyn®. Developed by duPont, Surlyn® is a plastic composition cover that practically cannot be cut, not even by an axe. The only trouble with these hard-cover (Surlyn®) balls is that they tend to peel, so most top golfers still prefer the soft-cover (Balata) balls. Nevertheless, the ball covered with Surlyn® is a good bet for the amateur hackers who tend to beat and chop the ball more often than they hit it. "I wish everyone used soft-covered balls," says one pro, "because I'd sell more balls that way. Some hackers now use the same hard-cover ball for three and four rounds. In fact, they generally use them until they lose them."

The ball covers of Surlyn® come in different thicknesses, too. For reasons of applied physics, the thicker the cover, the farther the ball will travel when struck by an iron, particularly when the ball has been set on a tee and struck dead-on. "The center of gravity is on the outside of that ball," observes one pro, "and it flies like crazy."

To make sure that no golf ball is too lively, Thomas has enlisted the help of an assistant, a super shotmaker named Iron Byron, whose swing is just like a machine's. In fact, Iron Byron is a machine, a mass of rods, shafts, bolts, cams, valves, springs, and cylinders assembled by a team of Ph.D.'s at the Polytechnic Institute of New York in Brooklyn. The robot-like device, which operates on compressed air, gets its name from having a swing programmed after that of Byron Nelson. With Thomas at the controls, Iron Byron can hit every type of golf shot, from a duck hook to a 400-yard drive straight down the middle.

When Thomas schedules his tests, the Ph.D.'s at Polytech ship Iron Byron to Far Hills, where Thomas anchors his robot in a pad of concrete in a building at the USGA's special testing range. The testing range cost the USGA more than $50,000. "It is absolutely flat from a hundred sixty yards out to three twenty-five," Thomas notes, "and it deviates from absolutely level by no more than two and a half inches. We maintain it like a competition fairway, too."

The USGA has decreed that when struck by Iron Byron, a golf ball should travel no faster than 250 feet per second, or about 170 miles per hour. Working with his scientists from Polytech, Thomas has developed another measurement: the Overall Distance Standard. The ODS has set a limit of 280 yards for golf balls struck by Iron Byron under a particular set of circumstances. Any greater distance and the golf ball is ruled ineligible. "The ODS," contends Arthur W. Rice, Jr., chairman of the USGA's Implements and Ball Committee, "will prevent any future arms race in golf balls. It also will assure that golf courses will remain as valid, difficult, and enjoyable five, twenty, fifty years from now as they are today."

Flouting the USGA's decrees, some manufacturers insist that their souped-up balls have a legitimate place in the market, and they continue to produce them in great quantities. However, it does not pay to defy the USGA. Before each of its sponsored tournaments, the USGA posts a list of golf balls that do not conform to its standards and, as such, cannot be used in the competition. The TPD maintains ball standards that are identical to those of the USGA.

Not that Frank Thomas, Iron Byron, the USGA, and the TPD are flawless. There is, of course, no way to test every ball, and ball makers have been known to slip up accidentally. In the Jackie Gleason-Inverrary Classic in 1975, Jack Nicklaus

An iron's clubhead is made from a ceramic mold (top), *which is heated to melt and drain the wax from the inside, after which molten steel is poured in.* Bottom: *Molds cooling after steel has been added.*

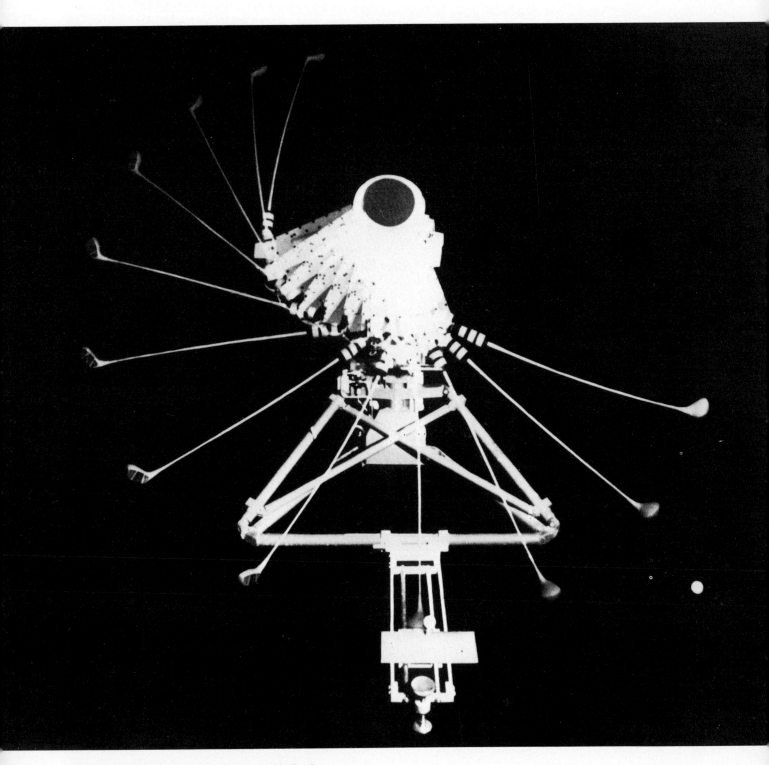

Above *and* opposite: *To test golf clubs and balls, the
USGA devised a contraption it calls Iron Byron, which produces
Byron Nelson's swing even better than Byron Nelson did.*

broke out a new ball as he stepped to the tee of a 185-yard par three. (He had been in a bunker on the previous hole.) Nicklaus could not decide on a club for the shot to the flag; it was either a hard seven-iron or a soft six. He finally took out the seven. He swung hard, and the ball seemed to take off with a roar. The shot carried over the green, over the rough, across a road, and, as far as Nicklaus was concerned, off into the sunset. Jack was stunned. He calculated he had hit the seven-iron more than 230 yards. So he put the club back into the bag, removed an eight-iron, teed up another new ball, and swung again. The eight-iron shot came up well short of the pin. "That new ball I hit had to be a rabbit ball," Nicklaus concluded. "I know that under the conditions I could not possibly have hit my seven-iron more than two hundred thirty yards."

The compression of a golf ball is simply a measure of how tautly wound up—i.e., how hard—it is. The compression of Nicklaus's rabbit ball was considerably more than 100, the compression rating preferred by most pros for their balls. Manufacturers generally try to make 90-compression balls, but the setting is unstable, and there are wide variations. The 90-compression ball you think you're buying may be an 85-compression or even a 95. Although the precise relationship between compression and distance is difficult to establish, it is safe to say that given the same swing, a 90-compression ball will not fly as far or as well as a 100-compression ball. On the other hand, the higher compression balls are somewhat more difficult to control. The ball Nicklaus hit on that par three simply had sneaked by the quality-control people at the golf ball plant.

All of which apparently goes to prove that despite the best efforts of Thomas and company, the manufacture of golf balls—and for that matter the equipment jungle in general—has yet to be tamed. The explosion of makes and models continues unabated, and the merchandising drivel flows in torrents. Iron Byron is valiantly plugging away, but he is clearly outgunned.

Opposite: *Molten steel being poured into ceramic molds.* Above: *Adjusting loft, the angle the shaft makes with the clubhead.* Left: *Coarse sanding of iron heads.*

Name		Score
		150
		152
		152
		157
		155
		151
		142
		WO Wesley
		143
		143
		152
		159
		150
		110
		111
		113

GOOBY	John	
COURTNEY	Chuck	
CRAMPTON	Bruce	
CRENSHAW	Ben	
CRISSY	Robt	
CURL	Rod	
DAVISON	Pete	
DENT	James	
DEVLIN	Bruce	
DICKINSON		
DICKSON	Bob	
DIEHL	Terry	
DOUGLASS	Dale	
EICHELBERGER		
ELDER	Lee	
ERSKINE		
EWING	Jack	
FERRIELL	Jim	
FEZLER	Forrest	
FINSTE		

3
A Slice of the Pro Life
Profile of a Tournament

It's a compromise of what your ego wants you to do, what experience tells you to do, and what your nerves let you do.

Bruce Crampton on tournament golf

They are some of the more affluent itinerant laborers in history, garbed in cashmere and polyester knits, performing at the most exclusive clubs. They are members of the Professional Golfers' Association (PGA) tour, and from January to November, from California to Connecticut, day after day and week after week, they work at a task that everyone else considers play. Through parched Arizona, sticky Georgia, sweltering New York, the essentials of their routine hardly vary: early rising and late practicing at the start of the tournament week, then four pressure-filled rounds in which to earn some money. And then it's on the road again, to Fort Worth, Texas, or Pensacola, Florida, or, in the case of the tournament to be examined here—the Kaiser International Open— to Napa, California.

To someone who has never tried it, this barnstorming around the country may seem like a cushy way to make a living. A pro golfer frequents posh country clubs replete with their wealthy members, flashy clothing, and flashier cars. There is no coach or manager to order him around. No one tries to throw a baseball at his skull or a punch at his nose. He rarely has to break a sweat.

Of course, it is not nearly that easy to be a pro golfer. First of all a player has to qualify. The PGA Qualifying School is a special brand of mandatory torture for all would-be pros. After attending several hours of classroom instruction on everything from dealing with the media to proper grooming, applicants play six to eight rounds of golf that determine everything. As few as 20 of the field of 300 do well enough to be accredited for the tour. The rest, unable to play on the pro tour but ineligible to compete as amateurs, may find employment in a pro shop or on the Far Eastern or European tours, where they will be able to work on their game until the next PGA School is held, in six to twelve months. The only other realistic option is to quit, while you are not too far behind.

Many of the pros have had to return to the PGA Qualifying School. Barry Jaeckel, a fine player from Los Angeles, missed qualifying more than once by only a stroke or two. Once, he lost out by a shot when he three-putted the final (one hundred sixth) green. He sat dazed and dumb in a corner of the scorer's tent afterward, looking like a man who had just lost his job, which of course he had. Jaeckel headed for Europe for several of the summers when he was ineligible for the American tour, and one year even won the French Open. Finally, in June 1975, he qualified for the PGA tour.

Whether they survive it or not, the golfers who compete in the PGA Qualifying School call it the most difficult week in their lives as golfers. And for the ones who do graduate, their problems have just begun.

Unlike a baseball or football player, who travels, eats, and lodges at his team's expense, a golfer pays for everything himself—room and board,

Beneath its veneer of opulence, the pro tour is a grind for most players. Opposite: The glazed beauty of a spring morning is lost on an early starter. Above left: At the Silverado Country Club in Napa, California, the Kaiser International tournament is a bit more leisurely than most.

After qualifying for the pro tour—often a harrowing struggle—a new pro must attract financial backing until he can support himself on his winnings. Ben Crenshaw was one of the very few sure bets for investors in golf talent.

laundry, transportation, entry fees (normally $50 per tournament), and caddie's salary, which ranges between $100 and $300 a week. Even under the grubbiest conditions—a subsistence diet of Big Macs and finger-lickin' chicken (which some golfers must endure)—it is impossible to play the tour without spending $20,000 a year. If the wife and kids are along, the figure doubles.

Few new pros can afford that expense, so the first order of business for a pro just out of PGA Qualifying School is to acquire financial backing. His sponsor may be a wealthy member of his country club, a few family members, or even one of those peculiarly daring investors who specialize in backing young pros. The golfer and the sponsor agree to a contract, usually of three to five years, whereby the sponsor receives a percentage of the golfer's income in return for footing the bill. There may be a clause enabling the golfer to buy out early, should he make it on the tour before the contract expires. More likely, he'll see to it that he has an option to renew.

If backing a Broadway play is the worst investment in the world, sponsoring a pro golfer surely ranks a strong second. It is certainly as unpredictable. Except for a prodigy now and then —a Jack Nicklaus or Ben Crenshaw—no one can spot the few who will make it. It is certain only that no more than a few will, so every sponsor's bet is a long shot. Someone calculated that in 1970 golf pro sponsors lost a million dollars. About the best that can be said for this type of investment is it is a rather reliable tax write-off.

Obviously, most of the touring pros are far from being a bunch of rich jocks jetting around the country to pick up a few thousand bucks for four days' play at another posh resort. It's more a matter of simply making a living, and travel is a lot less romantic with that as its purpose. Those who fail on the tour or merely survive take their lumps without much complaint (in part because there really isn't anyone to complain to who can do

much about it). Those who succeed feel that they're more than entitled to the good life. Golf is a game of the individual, and on the whole the pros are truly rugged individualists.

At all its week-long stands, this road show called the PGA tour depends on the efforts of a tournament administrator and his staff. For them, in direct contrast to the pros, a tournament is more like a year-long than a week-long event. Security forces must be hired, practice range balls purchased, programs prepared and printed, to mention only a few of the myriad of details to be attended to. After years of repetition, these chores are routinely and quickly handled, but at least one job, the most important one—of attracting a quality field—requires year-round attention.

There are nearly four dozen events on the PGA schedule each year. No golfer will play them all. All the pros realize that it is impossible to summon the enthusiasm and concentration necessary to play well in each of them. It's far better to go home periodically and take a week's vacation from dimpled white balls and undulating putting surfaces. Yet without the big names, a tournament can't hope to succeed. The spectators come to see the stars, so those are the golfers the tournament must have.

This makes for some tension between the weary lonesome travelers and their would-be hosts around the country. Tournament directors spend much of their year wooing the top pros with letters and personal visits. Since the golfers decide which tournaments to play and which to skip, the pro tour resembles the motion picture industry, whose producers corral big names for their films, rather than a centrally administered major league sport. Professional golf has adopted Hollywood's star system.

For Vern Peak, tournament director of the Kaiser International, time and location are the greatest factors in selling his tournament to the pros—time,

Every tournament strives to attract the celebrity pros because they assure a sizable gallery. Opposite: Fans too young to have seen Arnold Palmer in his prime can still have a mark of his success. Top: Jocular Lee Trevino. Above: Purposeful Tom Weiskopf.

mostly negative; location, wholly positive. The Kaiser is held each September at a resort complex called Silverado, in Napa, California. September is the warmest, most beautiful time of the year in northern California, but unfortunately it is also near the end of the pro golf season, which unlike the seasons of other sports, does not climax at the end. The highlights of the tour are the Masters in April, the U.S. Open in June, the British Open Championship in July, and the PGA Championship in August. By the fall, many of the pros are tired of golf. Those at the top of the money standings (invariably the same elite) don't even have a monetary incentive to continue, since once they earn $100,000 in a year, as they all have by September, the rest of their earnings goes to taxes.

To overcome these disincentives, Peak offers the pros who compete in the Kaiser some unaccustomed luxuries. At Silverado there are tennis courts, swimming pools, and, best of all to these itinerant laborers, condominiums to rent. A pro golfer's lodging is usually a Holiday Inn or a Travelodge. Jack Nicklaus or Arnold Palmer may rent a private home, but the majority of the pros, even those with six-figure annual incomes, stay in the same plastic-and-metal motels as the rest of America's travelers. Silverado offers a welcome change—bright white frame buildings with fireplaces. There will be no contending with traffic jams at the club entrance, no searching for parking places in a lot too small, no double cheeseburgers at the A&W stand.

Casting with the lures of his resort complex, Peak usually lands his share of the big fish. As the sky darkened over Silverado on the eve of the 1975 tournament, Peak could be reasonably satisfied with his catch. At the head of the field were defending champ Johnny Miller, Nicklaus, and Dave Hill, the pro who only a few minutes earlier had won the preceding tournament on the PGA tour, the Sahara Invitational, at Las Vegas.

Faces at the 1975 Kaiser—left to right: John Mahaffey, Dave Hill (winner of the previous tournament on the tour), and veteran Al Geiberger.

Peak had hoped before the 6 P.M. deadline to catch one or two more stars, Palmer or Tom Weiskopf, for instance, but then a few always get away, it seems.

Meanwhile, of course, all the other arrangements for the tournament had been made. Much of the work had been entrusted to volunteers. It had to be. A tournament with a $175,000 purse, as the 1975 Kaiser offered, usually costs more than $350,000 to hold. The additional money pays for security, staff workers, (tournament director Peak and a small crew of assistants), course maintenance, press and locker room food, fencing, and a variety of minutia. Without volunteer marshals, courtesy car drivers, scorers, and committee chairmen (many of whom earn more than $50,000 a year at their regular jobs), there would be no tournament golf. Jack Nicklaus might be running a pharmacy in Columbus, Ohio, and Hubert Green might be a salesman in Alabama.

The pro golf tour has existed in one form or another for half a century. Over the years an extensive manual has been compiled to guide tournament organizers in their preparations. There is a minimum length for flagsticks and a maximum length for grass on the greens. Positions for tee blocks and cup holes must be determined. But in the entire manual there is no mention of paying anyone except the pros. Volunteers are thanked verbally and, sometimes, with a free ticket or two.

Once, even the pros became volunteers, at least temporarily. At the close of the 1969 Michigan Classic, it was discovered that the $100,000 purse was nonexistent. Eventually, the PGA paid off all the money winners (including first-prize winner Larry Ziegler his $20,000). Since then the PGA has made certain that each sponsor has the purse in escrow long before the first shot is struck, as the tournament manual prescribes.

Monday, September 29, 1975, the first day of the 1975 Kaiser International tournament week, arrived as pristine as most northern California autumn days. Early that morning farmers went to work on the vines that produce California's best wine

grapes. Students left for school. Businessmen endured the commute to San Francisco, forty-five miles to the south. And a hundred or so unfavored members of the PGA tour played a round of golf at the John F. Kennedy municipal course in Napa.

Johnny Miller might still have been in bed in his mansion at Silverado. Jack Nicklaus might have been in Florida, closing one last business deal. These men were guaranteed spots in the Kaiser. But since no tournament has room for all the pros, only the better ones are granted the privilege of being exempt from qualifying. The rest have to compete against their fellow nonexempt colleagues for a place in the starting field.

After the PGA School and the struggle to obtain financial backing, gaining an exemption from qualifying is a pro's next great hurdle. There are 17 ways in all to become exempt from a particular tournament. The most common are: finishing among the top 60 money winners in a year, which gains the player an exemption for the entire next year; winning a tournament, which exempts the player for a period of a year after that tournament; and making the cut in a tournament, which exempts a player for the next tournament on the tour.

This week there were 42 spots open for nonexempt players, so the 42 low scorers at Kennedy would gain a place in the Kaiser. The setting was strictly proletarian. At a small coffee shop the pros' wives listlessly occupied themselves with sandwiches while their husbands played. Posted outside was a white cardboard rectangle on which Juel Isaacson, a Spalding salesman, kept the scores—a communal report card for a course marked strictly on a pass-fail basis.

Among the nonexempt players competing against each other this day was Joe Porter, formerly a fine amateur player and an all-American at Arizona State University. Porter had turned pro some six years before, at the urging of Tom

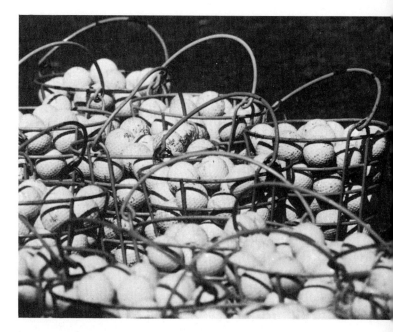

Opposite *and* above: *A cluster of spectators for a climactic moment on a green is even more ephemeral than a batch of baskets filled with practice balls.*

Weiskopf, a longtime friend. At the time Porter seemed a cinch to succeed as a pro, but he never won even a year's exemption and at least three times he left the tour to help manage his father's clothing store in Phoenix. Now he was back again, wondering, inevitably, if this time would be any different. "One thing is sure," said Porter as he awaited the start of the Kaiser, "I can't stay out on tour much longer like this. I've got to start playing better real quickly or get another job."

It's hard to be confident as a nonexempt player, or a "rabbit," as the nonexempt player is derisively called, because he is said to spend so much time in the "cabbage," that is, the rough. After the Monday round, the nonexempt player waits anxiously to see if his score is low enough to qualify him for the tournament. If it isn't, there might be a smaller, satellite tournament in the vicinity in which to play. But if, as in the case of the Kaiser, there is nothing else, the nonexempt player slams his clubs in his trunk (he's also called a "trunk slammer") and drives off in the direction of the next tournament. He'll try to find a site at which to play a practice round or two in preparation for the next Monday. Some pros go for weeks without qualifying for a tournament. And of course, qualifying for the tournament does not ensure qualifying for the final two rounds, from which the money winners are drawn.

In all, then, a golfer has four major barriers to clear before he can earn a living at this game: completing PGA School successfully; finding a sponsor; earning an exemption, and, finally, surviving the cut—the paring of the field roughly in half at the halfway point in each tournament to eliminate those who are out of the running.

This succession of barriers is both formidable in itself and in its psychological after-effects. After having invested so much just to have a chance to earn some money, many beginning pros are temporarily incapable of winning a tournament. "The way I look at it," says Johnny Miller, who

became one of the game's stars some four years after he qualified for the tour, in the spring of 1969, "everyone has a choking level, a level at which he fails to play his normal golf. As you get more experienced, your choking level rises. It really is very difficult for a new player to win because he's only worrying about, first, making the cut, then making money. You don't want to take many chances. You want to make certain you finish fifteenth or tenth or something like that."

Other athletes wear their names on their uniforms. Golfers, whose uniforms are more subtle, emblazon their names on their bags.

Consequently, rookie sensations are rare indeed on the pro tour—not because a rookie couldn't win, but because he is, in effect, afraid to try.

The entire qualifying method has been criticized as both unfair and psychologically degrading. The PGA has begun considering a new method of determining tournament eligibility, possibly to be instituted as early as 1978. There would be two tours—a major tour and a minor tour. For a fee anyone could play in the minor tour, and if he finished among the leaders after a two-month period, he would be seeded into the major tour. The poorer players on the major tour would be dropped into the minor tour. In the meantime the Joe Porters of pro golf struggle on.

On Monday Porter shot a two-under-par 70, and since par is invariably good enough to qualify, he knew he had succeeded for this week. Especially in the flush of these temporary victories, nonexempt golfers are apt to think of their troubles stoically if at all. Before he gained his exemption, Bob Wynn, a longtime rabbit, expressed the most prevalent rationalization. "Nobody put a gun to my head and made me come out here," he said.

There are only two golf events of note, the British Open Championship and the five-day, 90-hole Bob Hope Desert Classic, that begin on Wednesday. All the others start on Thursday. Tuesday, then, the day after travel (for exempt players), the day before the pro-am tournament (again, only for exempt players), is usually a time for relaxation and a lot of practice. A pro may spend hours on the driving range or putting greens. A favored preparation is pacing off yardage on the fairways, using sprinkler-system heads or the corners of sand traps as markers. In this way a pro gains easy reference points for determining how far a given shot of his has gone. Subtracting that distance from the total length of the hole, he knows just how far he is from the green and, hence, which club to use.

Despite these preparations, the mood is light, tension almost unnoticeable, especially in the warm weather and folksy atmosphere of the Kaiser. The focal point is the locker room. As clubs, shoes, and balls are unpacked and stored, the familiar tableau of golfers-in-repose unfolds. At the pool table, a favorite diversion at the Kaiser, Phil Rodgers, Jerry Heard, Rod Curl, Johnny Jacobs, and George Johnson are knocking out shots and stories. In a far corner Gene Littler, who recovered from a cancer operation and won several tournaments, including two during the year, is laconically rubbing the head of a two-iron and chatting with a sportswriter. Joe Porter, delighted to have made the starting field, grouses good-naturedly about missing another football game of his alma mater, Arizona State, and wistfully pictures the day when he'll have his exemption and be able to spend the fall doing nothing but watching Arizona State and Phoenix Suns games.

Dr. Gil Morgan, an optometrist who has chosen golf for the time being, discusses his prospects of making the top 60 money winners and thereby gaining an exemption for the next year, 1976. His chances don't look good, but he confidently plans to improve them with a good finish in the Kaiser and then another in the Texas Open. A few cackling laughs from the pool players reverberate through the room as Curl pockets a bank shot. As always, veteran Gardner Dickinson is complaining about his putting, despite the fact that at the practice green his stroke has been examined and pronounced quite healthy by a fellow pro.

So it goes. The locker room serves as something of a hideaway, where the pros can confide and commiserate in relative privacy. At the doorways are guards of the Burns Security Services to keep all but a few officials and the press outside, away from the players. The cozy comradery of the locker room is one of the few defenses the pros have against the inherent loneliness of their game.

That evening Jim Wiechers, who, in addition to Miller, Ron Cerrudo, and Rod Funseth, actually lives at Silverado when not on tour, invites some of his fellow pros and their wives to an annual wine party. Wiechers is part-owner of a San Francisco wine store with Tom Casazza, an old friend and now a neighbor, and he prides himself in knowing how to choose a vintage as well as he can charge a putt.

For the most part, pro golfers are not big drinkers. Usually they limit themselves to a guzzled beer or two, particularly after a round in the summer, and a cocktail before dinner. The 7:30 A.M. tee-off times and the ever-present demands for a delicate touch on the greens are incentives enough to stay sober.

At the Wiechers home this Tuesday evening, however, the guests are imbibing freely, of Pommard and Beaune from France, and pinot chardonnay and pinot noir varietals from California. Lee Elder, who a few months earlier had undergone the taxing experience of being the first American black to play in the Masters tournament, is sitting on a couch, in conversation, grasping a glass of white wine in one hand and gesticulating with the other. John Mahaffey and his blond wife, Sue, are sampling the hors d'oeuvres. And Tom Watson, the red-haired British Open champ and connoisseur of wine and politics, is ruminating over the 1976 presidential election, more than a year in the future. No one seems at all concerned about the Kaiser.

Wednesday is the day of the pro-am. For many of the amateurs it is one of the biggest and also most expensive days of the year. At the Kaiser, $750 buys an amateur a day of golf with a professional, mementos of the occasion, several tickets to the tournament itself, and the chance to win one or more trophies. Best of all, he can replenish his stock of conversational fodder, often to the dismay of his friends and acquaintances.

Tiresome as this bit of ego massage and status-seeking may be, there would be no tournament without it. In the 1975 Kaiser, for example, the amateur competitors (320) funded two-thirds ($240,000) of the tournament's total cost.

The amateurs are grouped three or four together with a pro, and their best-ball score, including the pro's, is recorded on each hole. In some

Top and above: *Golfers such as Joe Porter, who have qualified for the tour but not automatically for a tournament, live in a netherworld of Monday qualifying rounds.* Above right: *This fringe breed of golfer is known as a "trunk slammer," for the distinguishing mark of his arrivals and departures.*

tournaments (the Kaiser is one), the pro's gross score is kept also. An individual's low round in a pro-am wins $500, and the low team score another $500. There are lesser prizes for the other high finishers. So, even though he may be paired with several hackers, a pro does not approach this round without incentive. Nevertheless, most professionals consider the pro-am of value mostly as another practice round and as an opportunity to make valuable friendships. While helping some corporation vice-president or executive of a car leasing firm to select clubs, line up putts, and in general enjoy himself, a pro understands that someone who can afford to pay $750 for a round of golf with a pro often delights in lavishly returning a pro's favors when they are off the course.

Many pro-ams feature celebrity entertainers and athletes to hype the crowd. Joe DiMaggio or Jackie Gleason in a pairing draws as much attention as the name pros do. Gleason himself runs a tournament each February in Florida, and in 1975 he presented about as glittery a foursome as any star-gazer could ask for: Gleason, Bob Hope, President Gerald Ford, and Jack Nicklaus. Hope and Bing Crosby sponsor well-known winter tour tournaments that incorporate the pro-am into the tournament itself. But most pro-ams are only preludes to the tournament.

At the Kaiser the various companies within Kaiser Industries purchase a majority of the pro-am spots, for use by clients or home-office executives. Thus, the amateurs in the Kaiser pro-am are somewhat subdued in cast, if not necessarily in influence.

The pro-am, like the first two days of regular competition, is held on both of Silverado's courses, North and South. Golfers begin on the first and tenth tees of each course and, with luck, finish where they are supposed to five hours later.

Scheduled to begin at the relatively late time of 11:40 A.M., Jack Nicklaus consents to discuss his game with a newsman for a few minutes. The media has been overworking the Nicklaus vs. Miller story, Miller having dominated pro golf in 1974 and Nicklaus having regained prominence in 1975. In the twelve previous tournaments this year that both have entered, Miller has failed each time to finish ahead of Nicklaus. But Jack is interested in other things. He complains that now, close to his thirty-sixth birthday, he has lost distance on his shots. The extra 25 or 30 yards aren't there anymore when he needs them, he claims. A friend suggests that Nicklaus apparently doesn't need them. In the sixteen tournaments he has entered so far in the year, he has finished first, second, or third in nine of them. He has won five, and his $291,849 in prize money leads the PGA's list of money winners.

Another Nicklaus problem gains more sympathy. Angelo Argea, Nicklaus's regular caddie, has been suspended for a month for violating the rule that caddies are not allowed in the clubhouse. Argea entered the clubhouse at the World Open, in Pinehurst, North Carolina, after he was unable to attract Jack's attention outside. It was a bum rap, Nicklaus contends; the guard at the clubhouse door permitted Argea to enter. But a rule is a rule, Nicklaus concedes. So Johnny Miller has arranged for a college student and fine amateur golfer, Larry Cartmill, to carry Nicklaus's bag at the Kaiser.

In theory, anyone strong enough to haul 14 clubs, a leather bag, and a few towels for several hours should be able to caddie. But many of the pro golfers hire special, full-time caddies. A caddie can chart distances, analyze a swing, help line up shots (particularly putts), and, perhaps most important, become a much-needed, trusted constant companion. In golf, where so much depends on concentration, it benefits a pro to find a caddie who knows his pro's game and idiosyncrasies. The caddie disposes of minor matters before they become major ones and allows the pro to concentrate fully on each shot.

With Cartmill lugging Nicklaus's big

*Nicklaus meets the press. By an immutable law of the
media, every tournament must have pretournament drama,
and a golfer who is the tournament favorite, or at
least a leading contender, must play the starring
role. Nicklaus seems all too familiar with it.*

green-and-white MacGregor bag around the North Course, Jack shoots a one-under-par 71 during the pro-am. That puts him in a tie for fifth place individually (his team is out of the money), for which he wins $105, or about what a man earning $1 million a year would use for tips. Jerry Heard, having torn himself away from the pool table, ties Allen Miller and Bobby Cole for first place on the North Course with a 69. Al Geiberger, continuing the renaissance that he began a year earlier, shoots a five-under-par 67, low on the South Course.

Geiberger is not a man to invest too much responsibility in caddies. He likes to tell of the caddie he used to have who had two bad habits: drinking and persuading Geiberger to pay for it.

The caddie owed him so much money, Geiberger says, that whenever he had a chance to win a tournament he would choke. He just couldn't bear to think of where the money would go.

Geiberger has played in the Kaiser since its inception, in January 1968. He figures the tournament, like that caddie, owes him something. In January 1969, a heavy rainstorm hit Napa after the second round was completed. The third round, scheduled for Saturday, was postponed until Sunday, but the storm continued, and finally, on Monday, the tournament officials reluctantly canceled the competition, though there were still two rounds unplayed. Each contestant was paid exactly half what he would have been paid had he finished in the same position after four rounds.

If not yet a card-carrying occupation, caddying is
more respectable now than it used to be. Caddies are
not only invaluable consultants, *opposite*, *but*
sometimes personalities in their own right, as is
Angelo Argea, Jack Nicklaus's comrade, above.

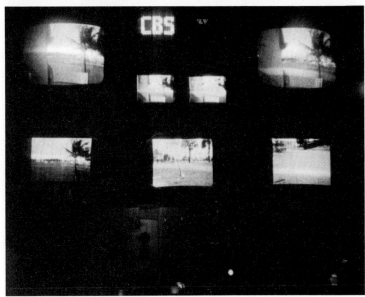

The central nervous system in television's coverage of a golf tournament is the trailer into which the many different camera shots are fed. But in reducing a sprawling course and tournament to some manageable rectangles, television can't capture the spectator's diverse experience.

Johnny Miller, the fair-haired boy wonder from northern California, captured the 1974 Kaiser International among many other titles in 1974, and now lives at Silverado. Opposite: It's a short commute from home (just off the eleventh green) to work.

Miller Barber received $13,500 for a 36-hole victory. Geiberger made $65.81. To stay the additional two days cost him some $150 in room and board. It was the first time, he mused, that he would have been better off missing the cut.

This sort of humorous storytelling is characteristic of the pro-am. But the next day, Thursday, the serious work begins, and already on Wednesday there are traces of a more somber mood. As a nonexempt player, Joe Porter is excluded from the pro-am, and thus from the chance to gain an extra practice round (as well as some extra pocket money). This is a particular problem at the Kaiser, in which both courses are used for the first two rounds. Having spent Monday qualifying and now Wednesday on the sidelines, Porter has had only one day, Tuesday, to familiarize himself with 36 holes.

Porter spends part of Wednesday knocking out a few buckets of practice balls. Finally, when most of the pro-am rounds are over, he and several other nonexempt qualifiers squeeze in a few holes before darkness.

Johnny Miller is king of the Kaiser. A native of northern California, he now lives in a $400,000, six-bedroom, redwood-and-glass mansion next to the pond near the eleventh green of the North Course at Silverado. During tournament time, he uses his private electric golf cart to get to the locker room area, but just in case the cart breaks down, there is a highly dependable Porsche Carrera in the garage. None of the four Silverado residents—Miller, Funseth, Wiechers, or Cerrudo—had done especially well during the tournament's early years. But Miller, at last, won it in 1974 and, particularly after his string of triumphs that year, became the undisputed hometown favorite.

But a tournament on your home course is not without irritations. There are friends and relatives stopping by to ask for free tickets. There is entertaining to be done. Early in the week there was a sports banquet and a fireside discussion with fellow members of the Mormon Church afterward. On pro-am day Miller had a commitment to make a brief promotional film for the 1976 Phoenix Open, where, in January, he

Watching golf is more tiring than it seems, left. Roaming a golf course in search of a tournament, a galleryite earns his grub, top, and relaxation, opposite. Above: *Standard equipment.*

would be defending another championship. After considerable preparation the cameras rolled and a smiling Miller invited an invisible audience to watch him play at Phoenix. The spot ended and a gray-haired director stepped forward and requested Miller to go through it again, only shorter this time, please.

There seemed a real danger that amid these minor distractions Miller might not work hard enough, particularly not on this course that he had played so many times and knew so well. Then too, he had the burden of having to explain why he had not so far this year come close to equaling his fantastic performance of the year before—eight tournament wins and a PGA record of $350,000 in winnings for a single season. By the time of the Kaiser, when he had won only three tournaments and $191,000, everyone was asking Miller what had gone wrong, though for anyone else, Miller's record would have been considered just fine.

"What I've done," Miller admonished before climbing back on his golf cart and heading home after the pro-am on Wednesday, "has bothered everyone but me."

Thursday brought the fourth straight day of perfect weather. Confident that their strong field and the promise of a Nicklaus-Miller confrontation would now bring out the fans en masse, Kaiser officials began to speculate about a record attendance. They were not disappointed. The fans surged into the Napa Valley from the two large metropolitan areas within an hour's drive, Sacramento and San Francisco. As the fans jammed the parking lots and crowded around the candy-striped tents of concession stands, they transformed Silverado from a subdued resort community to a teeming athletic arena. Every fine athletic contest thrives on the excitement of thousands of people massed to witness it—even a golf tournament, in which the galleries are dispersed. From the start the 1975 Kaiser had this key ingredient.

Golf fans are a strange and hardy lot. Spectating in most sports requires nothing more vigorous than sitting or standing in the grandstand. But the galleries at a golf tournament usually tour the course (in the case of the Kaiser, two courses) with the players. Drawn by the prospect of spending a day in the sunshine, of standing practically elbow-to-elbow with a star, of observing him play the way they cannot, the fans seem hardly to mind not knowing what is going on elsewhere. For keeping up with a tournament is almost impossible out on the course. There are usually too few scoreboards, and those few are often not nearly up to date. About the only exception is the Masters tournament, whose communications system is unquestionably the best on the tour. (It has to be. The crowds are so large, especially around the name players, that one can travel eighteen holes and never see a shot. But it's the finest tournament you'll ever hear.)

At most tournaments the pros begin teeing off before 8 in the morning ("dew sweepers" these early birds are called). Thus, by noon some golfers have concluded their rounds and their scores have been posted, whereas other golfers have yet to begin. At the Kaiser, however, a total of four tee-off points are used—the first and tenth tees on both courses—so that everyone can begin playing at a civilized hour, between 10 A.M. and 12:30 P.M. Since course conditions can change markedly over a long day (greens get trampled, it may begin to rain, for example), this system is probably the fairest. However, it means that half the field plays "backward" rounds (the back nine first, the front nine last), which destroys for these golfers what continuity an architect has built into the course. Moreover, the consolidation of starting times creates commuterlike congestion in the late morning. Golfers and caddies are everywhere—on the practice tee, on the practice green, walking toward the teeing area. The staccato click of spikes on the cement paths becomes a rumble.

A place for, clockwise from bottom left: *kindly gentility, a hearty lookout, dubious detachment, some serious sleeping.*

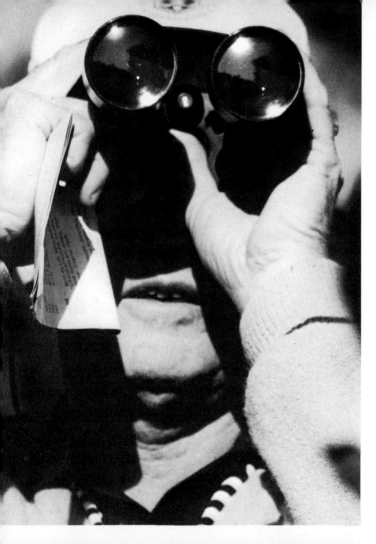

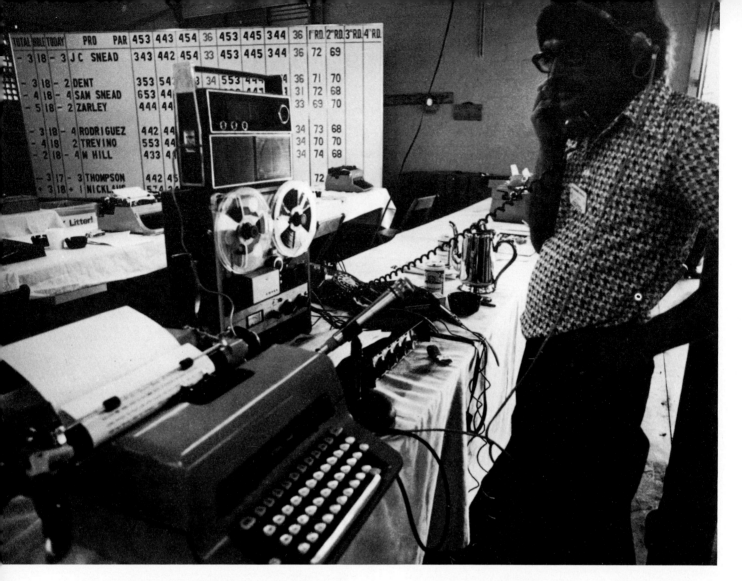

On the whole, however, the logistical benefits seem to outweigh the defects of confusion and the sin of breaking tradition. This is even a more sociable system. Amid the late-morning bustle, golfers have a chance to exchange greetings and wishes of good luck. Pro golfers are a most fraternal group of athletes, and it seems almost unnatural to send them off to their isolation on the course without allowing them at least a brief chance to mingle beforehand.

Joe Porter began his first round confidently, but he was soon in trouble. He was driving well, but the birdies weren't coming. As usual, he was having an awful time putting, the decisive factor in top-level play. "I've never putted well on the tour," he acknowledged. "The tougher the course, the better I usually play. My game is good from tee to green. But my putting is just fair to mediocre."

Porter finished with a mediocre 76, 11 shots behind the leaders, Gene Littler and Chuck Courtney, and in danger of missing the cut. Usually, the low-70 players qualify for the final rounds. On a difficult course and in bad weather, even the leaders may be around par, so the cut could be as high as seven or eight over par. But when the course conditions are excellent, as they were at the Kaiser, scores will be low and therefore the cut will be, too. After the first day, par had fallen so consistently that Porter calculated he would have to shoot no more than a 69 the next day in order to stay in the tournament.

Jack Nicklaus had an acceptable, if not wholly satisfying, day. He shot an even-par 72 and was told by a sportswriter, in a gesture more of

Above: The telephone and tape recorder rival the typewriter as a reporter's greatest aid. Opposite: Television set overlooks the press room at the Masters. Some golf writers cover a tournament without ever seeing a shot in person, and some golfers resent it.

diplomacy than expertise, that 72 wasn't such a bad score. (This was before either Littler or Courtney had finished.) "Are you kidding?" Nicklaus snapped. When everybody was in, he insisted, he would be far back. Sure enough, he ranked fifty-second after the first round.

This repartee between golfer and reporter took place, as similar dialogue during a professional golf tournament often does, in the press room. If golf is a difficult game to play, it is truly impossible to cover, especially when there are contestants starting their rounds simultaneously in four different places. To spare the writers the rigorous and often fruitless task of roaming around the golf course in search of a story, the leaders and/or the big names in a tournament re-create their rounds in the press room, usually over a soft drink or a beer. When they want to, the pros can display amazing recall. Without so much as consulting a scorecard, they can detail each shot—the lie, the distance, the club, the flight of the ball, everything.

However, golfers are so expansive only occasionally. Some resent the fact that many reporters will cover a tournament without ever seeing a shot. Ben Hogan once said scathingly, "If someone dropped an atom bomb on the sixth hole, the press would wait for a golfer to come in and tell them about it."

Other pros are just not disposed to linger over their rounds. At the 1970 British Open, Lee Trevino was orally racing through his round so fast that he skipped the eighth hole. He stopped and marveled, "No wonder I was able to shoot a sixty-eight."

Most of all, of course, the pros don't care to

relive their problems on the course. Such was the case with Nicklaus as he recounted his first round at the Kaiser. "I hit a drive and a seven-iron and two-putted from twenty feet," he began, summarizing the first hole. Five minutes later his 72 swings had been accounted for. At this point, as if to emphasize the uninspiring round, a minus-six went up on the scoreboard next to Courtney's name. Nicklaus regarded it without comment, paused for a few lighthearted remarks, then took his leave, eschewing the noisy locker room for his condominium near the first tee of the North Course.

Johnny Miller had cause to be more chipper. He had opened with a three-under-par 69, and he declared this the first occasion in weeks that he had played under control. There were three birdies and nothing close to a bogey. Content, he climbed aboard his electric golf cart and shuttled off with his eldest son, John, to the new homestead.

The biggest story of the day was, not surprisingly, the leaders, Littler and Courtney,

First-round co-leaders at the Kaiser International—Gene Littler, below, and Chuck Courtney, left. Littler would stay in contention through the later rounds; Courtney would not.

particularly Courtney because his success was so unexpected. He had won only three tournaments in his career, and his income from the tour had been so meager that at one point he had left the tour for a month. So the news media had a natural, if hardly unprecedented, story in his tying for the first-round lead.

Not that anyone was predicting victory for Courtney or, for that matter, Littler. In this way a golf tournament is like a distance race; the leader after the first lap is likely to be well back in the pack at the finish, or even after the next round. Such was Courtney's fate on Friday, in the second round. "Never found a fairway all day," he moaned after soaring to a three-over-par 75 and falling well off the lead. Littler did better, a 70, for a two-round total of 135, but even that was not good enough to keep him on top.

The leader after the second round was Don January, a lean, weathered Texan whose trademark is his golf shirt collar rolled up for protection against the sun. This day he had the hot putter and a record-tying eight-under-par 64 on Silverado's South Course.

A lot of sportswriters were mildly peeved at the new man's ascendancy or, at least, its timing. Trying to beat their deadlines, they had written some perfectly legitimate pieces on the impending battle between Miller and Lee Tevino, who were tied at 135 with Littler and Marty Fleckman after the second round, in what everyone assumed was first place. Then January birdied five of the last six holes and suddenly made all those stories useless.

The new leader smiled engagingly, trying his best to placate the rather disgruntled pack of newsmen before him. Grudgingly they recorded the details of his round and turned back to their typewriters to pound out the Don January story. It went something like this:

A few years earlier, while in his mid-forties, January had gone into what he described as semiretirement, returning to Dallas to build golf courses. With one boy already in college, he realized he hadn't much more time to be with his family while it was still together. But the economy turned sour, and real estate and golf course loans became impossible to get. January had no choice but to return to the tour. The first thing he noticed on his return was a lot of 22-year-olds who tended to call him Mr. January. The rest wasn't as flattering. Physically, his game was still sound, but his concentration had fled. In the middle of a tournament he would catch himself daydreaming about his family or business. He felt like a 46-year-old going back to college.

But January overcame. The week before he had shot consecutive 66s in the Sahara Invitational and finished in a tie for fifth. And now he was leading the Kaiser. It's nice to be back, he smiled.

For Joe Porter the Kaiser was over. He played considerably better the second afternoon than he had the first, but not nearly well enough. His even-par 72 left him at four-over-par 148 for 36 holes. He knew well before the cut was announced

that he wouldn't make it. If it was any consolation, at least he had spared himself the nerve-racking and rather degrading experience of waiting for the last scores to be posted and the cut-off point to be officially determined. At the end of the second round at every tournament, there are a group of borderline players hovering around the scoreboard, trying to stay calm and not to root openly against the late finishers. One man's score can alter the cut-off point by a stroke, which for the fringe men can be the difference between survival or elimination from the tournament. For those in this unhappy situation there is nothing to do but wait, hope, and try not to look like a vulture.

Spared such discomfort, Porter was in the locker room, disconsolately stuffing his golf spikes into his travel bag while half the field was still on the course. In a few minutes, after tipping the locker room attendant and saying so long to a few of the men he would see again next week in San Antonio, he climbed into his rented car and began the journey to San Francisco's International Airport.

The first Saturday and Sunday of October 1975 were a big sports weekend in northern California. In addition to the third round of the Kaiser, on Saturday there were two college football games—Stanford vs. Army and San Jose State vs. California—and the telecast of the first game of the Oakland-Boston American League playoff. Sunday brought two football games—San Francisco-Kansas City and San Diego-Oakland and the second American League playoff game, in addition to the final round of the Kaiser.

The golf tournament held up rather well against these other events, all of which generated some interest throughout the Bay Area. Indeed, they were widely followed at the Kaiser itself, by transistor radio and even through the tournament loudspeakers, which broadcasted the play-by-play of the pro football games on Sunday. These golf

Don January was the man with the hot putter and the lead in the second round. A late finisher, January miffed some newsmen because he outdated their early stories.

Interludes. Above: *Johnny Miller, right, pauses to fiddle and John Mahaffey to wait for him.* Right: *The orderliness of the game verges on symmetry as a threesome marks its scorecards and strides off the green.*

fans were obviously not just golf fans, but they were golf fans first.

There was little doubt about who they had come to see. Just one stroke off the pace, Johnny Miller had been playing well, and when Miller is playing well, his gallery is tremendous. Golf galleries are an anomaly among sports fans in that they usually root for the favorites. If an underdog in baseball or football wins, the fans celebrate. But if some rookie beats a Nicklaus or a Miller, he is apt to be rebuked. What did you do that for, kid? Perhaps it's the star system. Among the many pros, the fans can identify with only so many, and when some "virtual unknown" succeeds, he seems like an intruder.

Of course, in Miller's case his appeal was not only that of the favorite but also of the hometown hero. When it comes to expressing pride in the local product, golf boosters are no different from any others.

The threesome of January, Miller, and Trevino teed off on the North Course at 12:02 P.M. on Saturday before a huge throng. As the golfers followed their tee shots across the creek adjacent to the first tee, the big gallery surged after them. The last two rounds of the 1975 Kaiser were off to a big start.

After the cut, the field here, as in all tournaments, had been reshaped so that golfers with like scores would play together. The better the scores, the later the tee-off time. Thus, the January-Miller-Trevino threesome was the last to tee off. One hour ahead, and five shots behind, was Rod Curl, another northern Californian and the golfer destined to have the hot hand today.

At the start of the round Curl attracted a large gallery of family and friends, though not as large as Miller's. As the round progressed and his score began to rival the leaders', so did the size of his following. Curl shot a record-tying 64 and at the end of his round held the lead.

Out on the course Miller looked in astonishment

Late-round challenger Rod Curl, also a native Californian and resident of Silverado, attracted a gallery almost comparable to Miller's as he rose in contention.

at a scoreboard displaying a string of red, sub-par numbers extending beyond Curl's name. They showed six birdies and an eagle, and in the last column the net score, 12 under par. Miller was only 11 under.

Having held the lead and now lost it, Miller bore down. His 5-foot putt for a birdie on the seventeenth tied Curl; a 25-footer on the eighteenth regained the lead. Miller had shot his third consecutive round in the sixties, this time a four-under-par 68. After 54 holes he was at 203, a stroke ahead of Curl and Littler (still hanging in there), and three ahead of Fleckman.

So it came down to the final day. On the whole, the pros themselves are reluctant to predict the outcome of a tournament. But if a Miller or a Nicklaus is near or in the lead on the eve of the final round, one can hear the muted warnings around the locker room—watch out! Before the final round of the Kaiser, many of the pros were openly predicting, if not quite conceding, a Miller victory.

To put it mildly, Miller was due. In the first five weeks of the 1975 tour he had won three tournaments. In the six and a half months since then, he had won none. True, he had copped $191,000, which, as he had reminded everyone, hardly qualified him as a bust. Yet to anyone who had witnessed the torrid shotmaking of Miller in 1974 and early 1975, it was obvious that he could do better than he had so far this year. At the Kaiser he at last seemed ready to break out.

At noon Sunday, before what seemed like most of the record single-day crowd of 18,567, Miller began his final round. For the first nine holes he seemed determined to make a photo finish of this one. He stayed strictly at even par and led the field by only one shot, as he had at the start of the day. Then, finally, he summoned a finishing kick and, blond hair blowing in the wind, breezed home a winner. Three birdies on the first seven holes of the back nine broke open the tournament. He

finished the round three under par, at 69, for a 72-hole total of 16-under-par 272, three up on Curl and four better than Trevino, Fleckman, and Littler, who all tied for third.

And where was Jack Nicklaus during this Miller high life party? Well back in the pack, almost too far back to disrupt the scenario a bit. Afterward, Nicklaus munched on some popcorn and ruminated on the Nicklaus-Miller confrontation that never happened. If only he had applied a little pressure on Miller, made him work, Jack speculated. Then maybe John wouldn't have won. He might even have fallen apart.

No chance, retorted the ebullient winner. Jack Nicklaus was not going to beat John Miller this week no matter what, John said. It was a fair boast. The 1975 Kaiser belonged to Johnny Miller as surely as the sun shone on the grapes of the Napa Valley.

But the glow didn't last long. Even before the presentation of the top prize money the tour had already moved on. Hundreds of miles away, in San Antonio, Joe Porter and friends were preparing for their qualifying rounds the next morning, at the start of another tournament week. There the Miller victory at the Kaiser would seem far in the past, the Miller presence at Silverado very far away. Like roadside stops, golf tournaments appear and pass quickly. The changes in mood can become familiar and predictable, but they are too quick and relentless for comfort. The rhythm of transience is not soothing.

Above: The winner seemed pleased but hardly surprised.
Opposite: Likewise the family. A good tournament,
a sound win, but in the end to be remembered as just
another stop on an interminable tour.

4
The Swing's the Thing
Shotmakers

First, a little popular history, with apologies to golf's scholarly historians. Despite what all the PFC's in Arnie's Army have been told a few million times, General Arnold Palmer did not hit the first shot in the history of the game of golf. No, golf's first shot must be credited to some anonymous Scottish shepherd, centuries before Palmer enlisted the first recruit into his army. Tending his flock one day, the shepherd happened to take a poke with his crook at a pebble on the ground. It is not known whether he used an overlapping or an interlocking grip; where the ''V's'' of the grip pointed; whether he brought his crook back inside, outside, or perfectly straight; whether or not he paused at the top of his backswing; whether he kept his elbow in or flew it out; whether he spun or slid his hips as he moved through the ball; whether or not he executed a high follow-through with the club dead on target; and whether or not he kept his head down until after impact. Or, finally, whether his shot hooked, sliced, or went straight down the middle. But it's probably safe to assume that the innocent soul was blissfully unaware of all these matters. He may not even have noticed if his shot ever got airborne.

Not long thereafter somebody began to study what had become known as a golf swing, and not long after that, the continuing analysis of this intricate movement passed the point of diminishing returns. Today we have reached the stage where anything new or worthwhile to say about the golf swing is broached amid so much blather that one is tempted to call for a moratorium on the whole thing and wish for a return to the days of those Scottish shepherds knocking rocks around the linksland.

It seems that every professional worth his Amana hat, his crushed velvet leisure suit, and his whippy five-piece swing with a double loop at the top that collapses into a reverse twist at the bottom is spouting some new theory or, better still, ''revolutionary new theory'' about the golf swing, guaranteed to turn the 28-handicap hacker into a scratch shotmaker quicker than Lee Trevino can crack a one-liner. To make matters worse, many of these theories conflict with one another. For every pro who has discovered (always after a victory in some tournament) that the secret to winning golf lies in keeping your right elbow tucked in during the downswing, there's another who insists that the secret to winning golf lies in flying your right elbow out during the downswing. Contradictory though a lot of this advice may be, it is all selling.

A pro wins a tournament on a Sunday and by the following Wednesday he is either appearing at bookstores to autograph copies of his golf secrets, or, in case he hasn't yet put them in book form, sitting down with a tape recorder and rewrite man to do so, not knowing or not caring that it's all been said before, and probably in better prose. ''The fact of the matter is,'' says one book publisher, ''that all golf instructional books say the same thing. Oh, some players have gimmicks —short swings or long swings or in-between swings—but even they don't really believe those gimmicks. We had a player who wanted to do a book for us because he had discovered a new secret. His secret was that he completed his wrist break right there at the address position. Well, we went out and filmed him at a tournament, and if he completed his wrist break at address, I'm Arnold Palmer.''

Blame this propaganda proliferation on that evil machine, television. Before TV, golfers did not have to cope with an endless stream of mass-market advice. If Ben Hogan won the Los Angeles Classic by switching from a slight fade to a slight hook off the tee in the first round, nobody but his playing partners, a few people in the gallery, and Hogan himself were the wiser. As recently as the late nineteen-fifties, only some two million Americans knew something about golf, and only half that number cared about it at all. That

Television discovered pro golf at about the time that pro golf discovered Arnold Palmer. (Here he clinches the 1958 Masters.) Enticed by the Palmer style, millions of Americans took to the fairways and, naturally, became passionately concerned about their golf swings. The great golf swing craze is still with us.

129

Even Jack Nicklaus's swing deviates from the ideal, say the experts. However, they are quick to add that Nicklaus being Nicklaus, he compensates rather well, to to put it mildly, for the flaws in his swing.

was hardly enough to warrant a mass-media blitz.

Then television and a TV-star golfer named Palmer came along, and in about the time it took Arnie to hitch his baggy pants a few times, golf and Palmer had won a legion of followers, on the course and in TV land. As displayed by Palmer, golf was no sedentary sport for crotchety millionaires but a racy, risky game for everyone. No sooner would an ill-prepared announcer inform the television audience that "Palmer will probably lay up safe here," than Arnold would reach for a three-wood and bash a shot over the hazards and onto the green. In 1958, the American public discovered the Masters when Palmer won the tournament. Two years later he focused the country's attention on the U.S. Open when he charged from seven shots behind at the start of the final 18 holes and won the championship at Cherry Hills in Denver. By 1963, Arnie's Army was sizable enough so that when he blew the Masters with an unbelievable double bogey on the last hole, there seemed to be a period of national mourning.

Charged by Palmer's striking example, Americans by the millions took to the golf course. They wanted to do it the Palmer way, of course. Soon there were books, pamphlets, and daily newspaper strips telling them "how Arnold does it." And soon they were buying Arnold Palmer clubs and balls, wearing Arnold Palmer shirts, and getting their Arnold Palmer slacks cleaned at an Arnold Palmer dry-cleaning emporium.

Television began to dabble with slow-motion, stop-action, instant-replay, and videotape equipment, and that gave rise to the instant analysts. In some cases, to be sure, these expert commentators were really 28-handicappers from Madison Avenue, but soon television discovered knowledgeable analysts in golfers Byron Nelson, Dr. Cary Middlecoff, Ken Venturi, Dave Marr, and Bob Rosburg. They stopped films of swings to point out flaws or strong points, and suddenly, Americans who had been unaware of such

Recognized and respected practitioners of swing therapy— Conrad Rehling, opposite top left; Byron Nelson, opposite top right; and Jack Grout, above, ministering to Jack Nicklaus's son. Opposite bottom: Bobby Jones's swing.

subtleties as "the pause at the top," for example, were using such phrases to demonstrate their newfound sophistication. So here we are, deluged with more than any reasonable person would want to know about a golf swing.

This chapter proposes to survey the components of the best swings in golf, and in so doing, clarify the basics (if not reveal any secrets), according to those anonymous technicians behind the star shotmakers—the doctors of golf, as they like to call themselves. Have you ever heard of Conrad Rehling? Well, Conrad Rehling was the golf coach at the University of Florida who helped develop the swings of such professionals as Bob Murphy and Hubert Green, and he did the same as golf coach at the University of Alabama for Jerry Pate. Have you ever heard of Jack Grout? He is the man who taught Jack Nicklaus how to play golf when Jack was a youth growing up around the Scioto Country Club in Columbus, Ohio. Today, Nicklaus still visits Grout for what he calls "my annual checkup" (and for more frequent checkups, too). Not surprisingly, Nicklaus has entrusted his 14-year-old son, Jackie, to Grout for personal instruction. These doctors of golf know more about the golf swing than any touring professional.

As far as the doctors are concerned, there never has been and never will be the perfect golf swing. One teaching pro in Boston goes so far as to insist that he could "straighten out Nicklaus's swing in 10 easy lessons." What's wrong with Nicklaus's swing? Not much, of course, and certainly nothing important enough to require 10 lessons, easy or hard. Still, it isn't perfect, as we shall see. Like most pros, Nicklaus does some things that are "wrong" but that become right or at least harmless because he knows how to compensate for them. The rest of us aren't as fortunate, so these golf doctors strive for the perfect swing, realizing that unattainable though perfection may be, it is easier for them to try to teach the right way than to devise methods to compensate for the wrong way.

So here is that mythical perfect swing after all—the best part of the swings of the greatest players, the greatest shotmakers: Ben Hogan's grip, Byron Nelson's stance, Johnny Miller's hand position at address, Jack Nicklaus's position at the top, Sam Snead's downswing, Jack Nicklaus's leg action, Bobby Jones's sweep throught the impact zone, Sam Snead's follow-through, and Ben Hogan's finish. The composite perfect golf swing— one designed to win the Open, the Masters, and the PGA all in the same week.

And, by way of contrast, here is what the greats do "wrong," or at least what the swing doctors rarely prescribe for their practice-tee patients, despite, again, the success of the stars who have these peculiarities: Sam Snead's or Arnold Palmer's grip, Lee Trevino's stance, Jack Nicklaus's head position, Arnold Palmer's takeaway, Ben Hogan's position at the top, Jack Nicklaus's downswing, Arnold Palmer's leg action, Byron Nelson's dipsy-doodle through the impact zone, Johnny Miller's follow-through, and Johnny Miller's finish.

Grip

Basically, there are two grips: weak and strong. With a weak grip the "V" formed between the thumb and the index finger of your left hand points more or less to your left shoulder, never to your right side. With a strong grip the left hand is set across the grip so that the "V" points in the vicinity of your right shoulder. The weak grip is a fader's grip; the strong grip is the hooker's grip. With a weak grip the back of the left, leading hand necessarily faces the target and, in essence, keeps the clubhead on target. With a weak left hand, it is almost impossible to turn your right hand over the left at impact and thus create a galloping hook. With a strong grip, however, your hands do roll over, the right crossing over the left as you move through impact. The clubhead strays from the desired square-to-the-target plane, cuts across the

Compared to men, most women have greater strength in their legs and hips than in their upper bodies. Laura Baugh is no exception. Thus, her backswing, above right, is less important and intense than her follow-through, opposite.

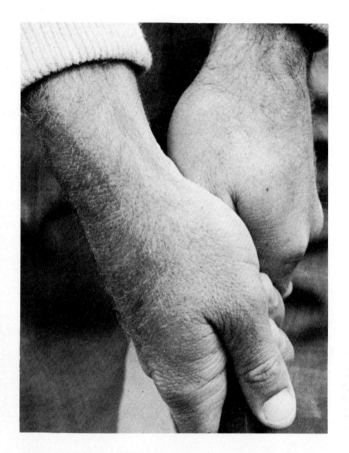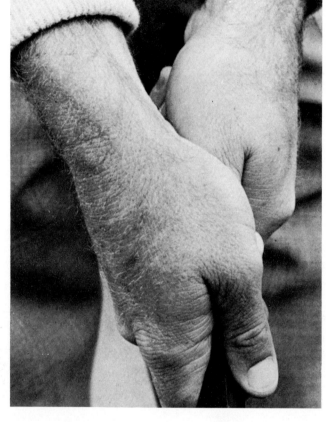

ball, and produces a hook. This flaw that results from a strong grip is particularly harmful in bunker play, for if the right hand crosses over the left, the club will bury in the sand and the ball will likely fly out of the bunker into orbit.

With few exceptions, most notably the modern-era players Arnold Palmer and Sam Snead, the great majority of golf's great shotmakers have always preferred to hit the ball with a distinct fade rather than any type of hook, ranging from "draw" to "galloping" to—yeeks!—"duck." The fade is a tightly controlled shot, whereas the hook is too often a wild, boundless one. The faded shot rises majestically off the clubhead, slides slightly from left to right as it reaches its peak, then falls serenely, bounces once or twice, and comes to

rest. A hook, on the other hand, shoots off the clubhead on a right-to-left course, skims wickedly along instead of peaking gracefully, lands with barely diminished speed, and darts away on a long, long roll. Not the sort of shot conducive to a steady, controlled game. "If I never hit another hook," Lee Trevino, a fervent fader, once said, "it will be too soon."

For years Ben Hogan hooked the golf ball, and during that time he enjoyed only moderate success as a touring professional, though he did win the 1948 U.S. Open at Riviera in Los Angeles with his hook. When he decided to rid himself of the hook forever and play only a fade, Hogan began to tinker with his grip. He placed the left hand on top of the shaft, not around it, in the weak position. By adopting the weak grip, Hogan

In a strong grip, above left, *the "V" formed by the thumb and index finger of the left hand points toward the right shoulder, whereas in a weak grip,* above right, *it points toward the left shoulder.* Opposite: *In sand a strong grip is particularly hazardous. Bruce Crampton's grip is about neutral here.*

eliminated most of his erratic shots and he learned how to hit a controlled fade with amazing consistency (that is, on almost every shot). Using the new approach, he won the U.S. Open in 1950, 1951, and 1953. He became so taken with the fade that he had difficulty hooking the ball even on those rare occasions when a hook was absolutely necessary. "Ben Hogan would rather have a coral snake rolling inside his shirt than hit a hook," observed Claude Harmon, a great touring pro and later one of the game's most respected teachers as the head professional at the Winged Foot club in Mamaroneck, New York.

The golf doctors are so confident in their belief that the weak grip is the proper one that they criticize even Sam Snead's swing, perhaps the prettiest in the history of golf, because Snead employs a strong grip. At times Sam's grip produces the dreaded galloping hook, the good doctors insist. They readily concede that the rest of Snead's swing is solid and that, moreover, he has built in a number of safeguards to compensate for the flawed grip. But flawed it is, even if Snead has won the most tournaments in the history of the pro golf tour and, at the age of 60-plus, still plays a highly respectable game on the pro tour. The notion persists among the technicians that Snead might have been the greatest player in history, not just the sweetest swinger, if he had altered his grip, like Hogan did, when he was a youngster.

There is one great variable in this perennial hook-versus-fade issue, however—the golf course. Some courses favor faders; others help hookers. It is no coincidence that Nicklaus, who prefers to hit a high fade, has passed up a number of events on the tournament trail when the course was one that favored hookers over faders—the Pleasant Valley Club in Sutton, Massachusetts, for one.

Ideally, a golfer could switch his swing to suit the course. Unfortunately, that doesn't work. The hook and the fade are drastically different shots, requiring distinctly different swings (the grip being

Arnold Palmer does many things "wrong." His too-quick swing makes for a less than balanced finish, opposite. His strong grip produces draws verging on hooks, and some anxiety, above.

Above: *Byron Nelson's seemingly stiff but almost pendulumlike takeaway flows from an ideal stance.* Right: *Lee Trevino effects a straight takeaway despite a wide-open stance.* Opposite: *Palmer's head anchors his magnificently powerful swing.*

*At the top—Gary Player, left; Ben Crenshaw, below;
Jack Nicklaus, below left. The higher the hands,
the more powerful the swing, but if the hands go
too high, they tilt the club well past parallel
and jeopardize the balance of the swing.*

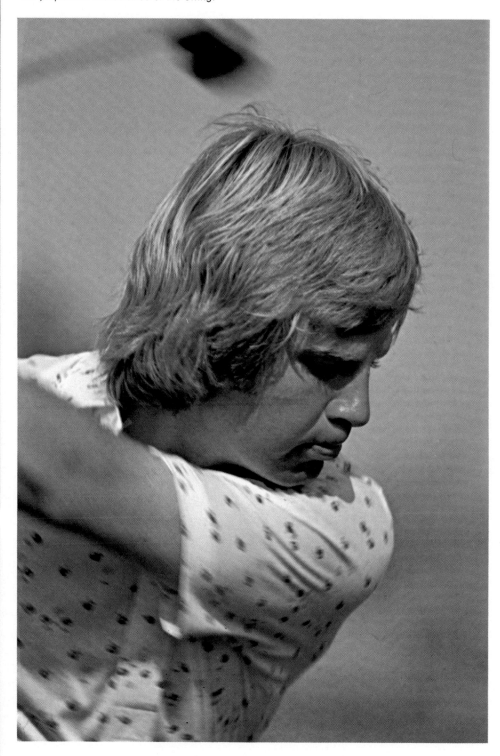

only the most obvious point of departure). And the delicate, intricate, interdependent system that is a golfer's swing pattern cannot easily accommodate such profound change. Jack Nicklaus learned this lesson at the 1975 U.S. Open, played outside Chicago at the Medinah Number 3 course. For several weeks before the tournament, Nicklaus practiced a hook-type tee shot because on several holes Medinah gives distinct advantages to the hooker. All went well for 69 holes of the Open, and as Nicklaus stepped up to the sixteenth tee of the final round he had a strong chance to win the championship. The sixteenth should have been a natural for Nicklaus—Nicklaus the fader, that is. It is a par four of slightly more than 450 yards that demands a faded tee shot begun along the left corner of the rough and turned back to the middle of the fairway. So what happened? Nicklaus duck-hooked the ball into the left woods, and, well, good-bye U.S. Open. "I wanted to hit a shot I had hit perfectly a million times," Nicklaus said later as he groped for an explanation. "That is my bread and butter shot, the kind of left-to-right drive that I've hit ninety percent of the time the last twenty years. Only this time I dead pull-hooked the ball into the trees. I knew immediately where it was going. . . . I just made a mental mistake."

Hookers and faders alike, take note: trying to change from one to the other for one hole is a hazardous prospect at best, even for a great shotmaker.

Stance
There is no sliding from side to side in the perfect swing; it is just a simple backward and forward motion, like a pendulum—two-dimensional. Of course, a real golf swing is necessarily three-dimensional, as inevitably three-dimensional as the golfer himself, but other things being equal, the closer he gets to a pendulum-style swing the better. To achieve it, the stance is crucial. An upright stance, with the ball close to the feet, creates it. It forces the golfer to bring back the club perfectly straight and then down and through the ball on the same, perfectly straight plane (two-dimensional). Byron Nelson, the man whom most modern-day golf enthusiasts know as the swing analyzer, had just such a stance and the fine swing it produced. He was so upright as he addressed the ball that he looked rather stately, almost stiff. Call it neat; the record 11 straight tournaments he won on the pro tour one year were nothing less.

One other point about stance. A popular theory in golf has been that the shorter the club you are using, the farther back the ball should be in relation to your stance. In fact many players position the ball almost off their right toe as they prepare to hit a pitching wedge. Jack Nicklaus is one great exception. He plays all his shots, with the possible exception of some bunker explosions, off the heel of his left foot.

Hand Position at Address
The left hand is the key. By keeping it well forward, sort of pressed ahead of the ball, with the back of it facing squarely at the target, a golfer almost ensures a solid hit. Johnny Miller, the roaringest young lion on the tour, does this best. His left hand is square and solid at address, allowing his right to flail away as he strikes the ball.

Head Position
While readily conceding the fact that Arnold Palmer reigned as the king of golf for almost a decade, a lot of golf doctors today continue to believe that his swing has more flaws than any 32-handicapper's. They like to point out that Palmer's grip is too strong, which it is, and that he swings the club too quickly, which he does. Of course, they also like to mention that he has won a couple of million dollars and trades in his old private jets as most people trade in their used economy cars. What has saved Palmer, or so the

Johnny Miller's explosive swing begins with a windup that takes the club past parallel at the top, above. *At impact the left hand functions to control, if not restrain, the tremendous forward momentum,* left.

doctors believe, is his solid head position throughout the swing. "If Arnold ever gets around to moving his head, like the rest of us," says one touring pro, "all those semicontrolled hooks he keeps hitting will become galloping hooks overnight."

The head is the anchor of the swing. From the address through impact, the golf swing requires that every part of the body move—every part, that is, except the head. For if the head moves, if the anchor moves, the rest of the body will be very difficult to control. A surprising number of pros (a majority) tend to alter their head position, however unconsciously, during their swing. Nicklaus, for one, had a rather pronounced head movement in his early days in golf. He was cured when his mentor, Jack Grout, had an assistant hold Jack's head in place throughout the swing, but Nicklaus still cocks his head slightly as he begins his backswing. Not Palmer. As he attacks a golf ball, it appears that his head is set apart from the rest of him, almost as if he is afraid to move it. And if the swing doctors are right, he should be.

The Takeaway

Lee Trevino plays with what Texans like to call a "caddie hustler's swing." His stance is so wide open that it seems as if he will be able to hit only the unmentionable shank. However, Trevino keeps the golf club unbelievably square as he brings it back from the address position, and by abruptly shifting his weight to his left side and swiveling his hips on the way down, he eliminates the danger of a shank, which is inherent in the wide-open stance for everyone else. In effect, Trevino creates the pendulum that Nelson's stance makes almost automatic, and Lee's almost awkward. It appears to the untrained eye that Trevino isn't taking the club back straight at all, but he is—solid and straight, with the club square on target. No outside-inside pulls; no inside-out blocks.

In sum Trevino works with tremendous balance

Looking from the ground up at Johnny Miller's swing may be the best way to see its power and his trancelike immersion in it.

147

and the smoothest transfer of weight in golf today. He experiences difficulty only when he tries to keep up with longer hitters and, thus, overswings. He also employs his hands better than most players, imparting tremendous spin on his shots by cutting the ball with a slick hand movement as he moves through the shot.

Position at the Top

In general, the higher the hands at the top, the more power to the swing. Nicklaus keeps the club very high at the top, sometimes moving it past parallel to the ground. In contrast, Hogan's hands were too low at the top of his swing, his club too ''flat,'' in swing doctor parlance. Of course, the height-of-the-hands factor can be overstressed, and, in fact, Johnny Miller seems to. He is so distance-conscious that he often goes well past parallel at the top, the start of problems later in his swing.

Downswing

Mainly a matter of smoothness and coordination. Snead has always had a picture-book swing—a long, lean, powerful, yet seemingly effortless motion. Hogan too had a beautiful swing. Nicklaus's, on the other hand, is quirky; Palmer's almost abominable. Though Jack stubbornly denies it, there is evidence that he allows his right elbow to stray outward on the backswing and

The Snead swing in 1955. (It's not much different today.) Except for an overly strong grip, the swing doctors find nothing here that differs from their hypothetical ideal.

remain out during the downswing—the sort of thing that leads to an outside-in swing for mortal golfers. Palmer's sudden, jerky, wrenching movement is almost the antithesis of smoothness and coordination.

Leg Action

Leg action is what gives Nicklaus his consistent power. He glides through the ball with terrific force, generated mostly by the legs. And yet all the time he manages to maintain his balance, which Miller, for one, is not always able to do. After going well beyond parallel at the top of his backswing, Miller seems to leap into the ball (and almost out of his shoes). He then follows through to an

unsteady finish. A blend of power and balance, then, is the key to the success of Nicklaus, apart from the fact that he no longer tries to drive the ball prodigious distances, striving for pinpoint accuracy instead.

Swing through the Impact Zone, Follow-Through, Finish

Bobby Jones, who played with hickory-shafted clubs, had a big, slow swing, and often he went past parallel himself. However, he recovered well and seemed to sweep the club through the ball. He got plenty of overspin as a result. "Jones swung too closely and looped the club a bit at the top," one critic said, "but he probably had to swing that

Left: *Lanky Hubert Green seems to tower even taller as he finishes.* Below: *Jerry Heard keeps his head fiercely down.* Opposite: *Mike Hill labors to escape the rough.*

way because of the unknown quality of hickory shafts." Jones's sweep through the ball was a joy to watch: he glided through the shot with the grace of a dancer. Nothing jerky, nothing superfluous, nothing unexpected. (In contrast, Byron Nelson used to dip his hips on impact—at best a superfluous accessory to his swing.) For Jones everything was carefully studied, analyzed, tested, and refined. And of course it worked. Inevitably, he had a fine follow-through and finish too, like any graceful swinger. Snead's follow-through was flawless, too, demonstrating perfect extension and balance. Hogan's finish was tops, the club perched serenely on top at the end.

Compare the easy, natural finishes of Ben Hogan, above left, and Sam Snead, above middle, with the twisted form of Arnold Palmer, above right. Opposite top: Short, slight Buddy Allin virtually wraps the club around him at the finish. Opposite bottom: Big hitter Jim Dent can afford a high finish.

Who then has the best swing of all? Strange as it may be, he has not been mentioned in the preceding rundown. He is Tom Weiskopf, and his fluid, pendulum-like swing is almost a work of art. Unfortunately for Weiskopf, the rest of his game doesn't do justice to his swing. His failure to think soundly and to keep his temper on the course has plagued him, and he has yet to emerge as a truly great player. "Some day Tom will put it all together," predicts one touring professional, "and when he does, it will be all over for the rest of us. He has more talent, more natural ability, than most of us have put together."

Obviously, the golfer with the best swing is not

necessarily the best shotmaker. As mentioned earlier, there is no perfect swing. The test of a shotmaker comes not in some theoretical analysis of his typical swing, but in his swing under pressure. To understand this concept fully, it is necessary to digress a bit here and discourse on the peculiar marriage of those two partners in shotmaking—luck and skill.

In 1976, Roger Maltbie won the first Memorial Tournament at Jack Nicklaus's superbly designed Memorial Course at Muirfield Village in Columbus, Ohio, with the help of a shot that was 100 percent luck and 0 percent skill. Locked in a three-hole, total-strokes playoff with Hale Irwin, Maltbie pull-hooked his mid-iron approach to the green at the second playoff hole, the seventeenth. The ball seemed certain to come to rest deep in the thick, wiry rough on the hillside to the left of the green, from which point the recovery shot would require Maltbie to cut through the wiry grass with his sand wedge, pop the ball into the air, and land it on the fringe, with the hope that it would stop within makable putting range, which at Muirfield means about six inches. In other words, Maltbie seemed destined for a bogey, perhaps a double bogey, while Irwin, who had played his second shot comfortably onto the green, could confidently anticipate taking home the winner's check of $40,000. But in the few seconds that it took Maltbie's ball to reach its destination, everything changed. No sooner had Maltbie banged down his club in disgust after hitting the shot than he watched a miracle. The ball crossed the front of the green en route to the rough, scattering the spectators behind the rope, then, unbelievably, struck one of the rope-support poles dead-on and ricocheted at a 90-degree angle toward the hole! It landed on the fringe and rolled down toward the cup, finally stopping about 15 feet away. From there Maltbie two-putted and remained in a tie with Irwin.

Clearly, there is a point at which the

all-important swing becomes all but irrelevant. Maltbie blew the shot and, as it turned out, won the tournament. For on the next hole, Irwin pushed his tee shot into the edge of the rough right behind a tree and had almost no shot to the green. In fact he bent the shaft of his club in trying to punch his shot toward the green, only to send the ball into the same type of thick, wiry rough that Maltbie's shot should have found on the previous hole. What a way to go! For winning, Maltbie received not only the $40,000 first prize but, from a thoughtful Jack Nicklaus, the pole that had saved his shot at the seventeenth green.

In this case there was no confusing luck and skill. Usually it's a little more difficult to distinguish the two. Even old Gene Sarazen would have to admit today that there was a lot of luck in his "shot heard 'round the world"—the magnificent double-eagle he made at the 485-yard, par-five fifteenth hole at Augusta National in the 1935 Masters, a shot that tied him with Craig Wood and precipitated a playoff the next day that Sarazen won. The question here is not how much luck but how much skill. Of course, it goes without saying it was a splendid golf shot, indeed a perfect one, but was it, as old-timers insist, "the greatest pressure shot" of all time? Hardly. After all, at that point Sarazen was three strokes back with four to play—more a hopeless situation than a pressure situation. He had little choice but to play for the

pin. Pressure comes when a golfer finds it difficult to balance the risks of a given shot against its potential value. For example, a golfer one stroke behind with four holes to play cannot afford a disastrous mistake, and yet at the same time he must take some risks to put himself in position for the birdie that will tie him for the lead. The balance becomes even more delicate, the pressure ever greater, when a player is nursing a narrow lead through the final holes of a tournament.

Touring pro Bob Murphy has said, "It's not how well you hit the golf ball but how well you miss it that counts"—in other words, how close to perfection you can get, realizing that only luck can (but usually won't) do the rest. The ultimate skill in golf is confronting this unsettling truth under pressure—making important, and very likely questionable, strategy decisions about what sort of shot to attempt, then executing the swing properly despite the pressure. Or, as Toney Penna put it, "Everybody has two swings: the one he uses during the last three holes of a tournament and the one he uses the rest of the time."

In the 1975 Masters, Jack Nicklaus entered the third round leading by five strokes. He ended the day trailing the leader, Tom Weiskopf, by one, but he still seemed confident he could win. Asked about his prospects, Nicklaus grabbed his neck, laughed, and replied in falsetto, "When we come down to the final holes, some people find it very . . . hard . . . to breathe." It was hard to interpret that remark as anything but a prediction that someone other than Nicklaus would choke at the finish the next day.

Sure enough, with just four holes to play, Nicklaus continued to lag a stroke behind Weiskopf. On the fifteenth hole (the same one, with slight modifications, that Sarazen had double-eagled in 1935) Nicklaus crashed a drive down the middle of the fairway, leaving him, by his calculations, 242 yards from the flag stick. When Nicklaus says he has a given number of yards left

to the green, be it 242 or 963, believe him. When it comes to shotmaking, he knows everything down to the wind-chill factor.

Nicklaus elected a one-iron and hit what he called at the time "the best pressure shot of my life." The ball floated over the water in front of the green, touched down on the putting surface, and rolled to a halt within 15 feet of the cup, from where Nicklaus two-putted for his birdie. But Weiskopf didn't crack. He also birdied the hole, thus preserving his one-stroke advantage. The struggle continued to the sixteenth hole, a par three over water to a long green with bunkers in the rear.

Nicklaus hit a poor mid-iron to the green; the ball backed off a mound and came to rest approximately 40 feet from the hole. It did not seem to be the sort of putt to go for, not in the final round of the Masters, not when you are one shot behind the leader. Being bold here seemed nothing less than being stupid.

Playing in the twosome behind Nicklaus, Weiskopf had reached the sixteenth tee now, where he watched Nicklaus standing over the ball. Nicklaus drew back his flange and struck the putt. The ball rolled up the hill and began to turn to the left toward the hole. When the ball was 10 feet from the hole, Nicklaus crouched in anticipation with his putter held high in his left hand. The ball made one final curl, then dropped into the cup. Nicklaus leaped into the air, tap-danced around the green, shook both arms in triumph, and raced off to the seventeenth tee. Back on the sixteenth tee, Weiskopf suddenly looked depressed, though not as depressed as he looked a moment later, when a poor mid-iron off the tee and an equally poor chip shot left him with a 20-foot putt he failed to convert for a par. Suddenly, Nicklaus was in the lead.

He finished with deliberate pars, carefully hitting his tee shots into the safest fairway positions and, with equal care, sending his approach shots to

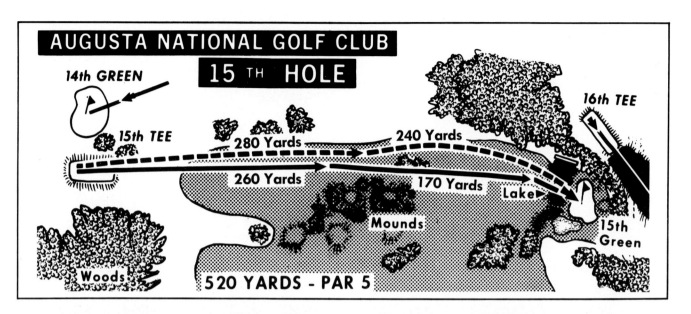

To judge true shotmaking skill, look at the pressure situations.
Top: *In the final round of the 1975 Masters, Jack Nicklaus reached the fifteenth green in two (dotted line) instead of the conventional three (solid line) with a spectacular one-iron. On the next hole he sank a 40-foot putt (above left and right).*

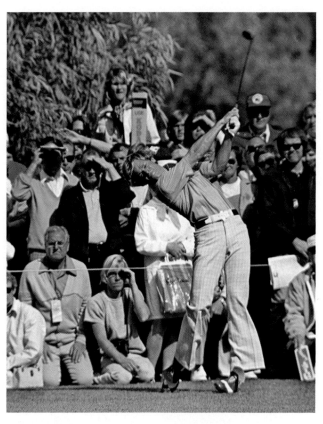

The arsenal of the ideal shotmaker would include
the driving game of Johnny Miller, top right, *the short irons
of Gary Player,* above right, *and the middle irons and
sand play of Lee Trevino,* above.

Jack Nicklaus is the long-iron king of today's shotmakers and, many would argue, the all-around king as well.

positions on the green from which he could easily get down in two. Weiskopf had a chance to tie Nicklaus at the eighteenth, but his 10-foot putt for a birdie slid just by the right edge of the hole.

Point of the story? Weiskopf may not have choked, but Nicklaus played more confidently, and more successfully, under pressure.

One more example of such extraordinarily poised shotmaking illustrates playing with grace under pressure, the ultimate skill in any sport. Standing beside his ball in ankle-high rough on the seventy-second and final hole of the 1976 U.S. Open at the Atlanta Athletic Club, rookie Jerry Pate realized he had to get the ball onto the green and then down in two putts for a par in order to win the championship. A strong order for a Nicklaus, not to mention a rookie pro, because the ball was resting in front of a clump of onion grass in such a way that the golfer would have to pick up the club sharply on the backswing and then hit the ball fairly cleanly, almost chopping down on it to avoid the clump of grass. Pate had to hit this shot approximately 190 yards, avoiding water in front of the green and to the left, and deep sand traps seemingly everywhere else. He decided on a four-iron. "No," his caddie advised. "Hit a five." The caddie reasoned that the lie was such that the ball would fly out of the rough; moreover, he calculated that his golfer was so wound up emotionally that Pate would get at least four-iron distance from his five-iron. Pate took his caddie's advice and the five-iron, and hit one of the greatest shots in Open history. The ball flew out of the rough, just as the caddie had predicted, carried the water beautifully, and fell just below the pin, finally coming to rest less than three feet away. Pate made the birdie putt and the Open was his.

On that inspiring note, our examination of the golf swing concludes. There remains the matter of breaking down shotmaking into the various shots and detailing the secrets of each. Unfortunately, it is impossible to cover here the many techniques that make a given man superior with a given club. Each great has written extensively about his skills and posed for thousands of pictures that illustrate them. Suffice to say that the modern-day composite superstar would have Johnny Miller's driving game, Jack Nicklaus's long irons, Lee Trevino's middle irons, Gary Player's short game, and the bunker games of, oh, Player and Trevino.

And here is only one of their more worthwhile tips: Player's "secret" to his exceptional short-iron play. (In general more golfers win tournaments because they have mastered short irons rather than the longer clubs.) Most golfers tend to sway too much as they attempt to play the little, finesse shots to the green. Consequently, they scalp the ball and line it over the green, or shank it into the woods, or just plain chili-dip it a few feet forward. To eliminate the chance of sway, Player determinedly plants his right foot against the ground in such a way that the outside of his shoe is actually off the ground. In effect Player creates a mound of resistance against which he presses during his swing. His immobilized right foot holds the rest of his body immobile. Player practices much the same technique in bunkers.

How good is this composite shotmaker Miller-Nicklaus-Trevino-Player? Well, throughout the end of the major-championship season of 1976, he had won a total of seven U.S. Opens; six British Opens; seven Masters Championships; eight PGA Championships; 200 or so other titles in events ranging from the American Golf Classic in Akron, Ohio, to the South African Open to the Piccadilly Match Play Championship; more than $10 million in a combination of dollars, francs, lire, pesos, pounds, and other currency. But remember one thing: Miller-Nicklaus-Trevino-Player has yet to execute the perfect golf swing.

5
Putting:
Of Mind and Body

An engineer recently calculated that putting is 43 percent of the game, thereby assuming that it *is* part of the game, perhaps because it requires the use of a club and a golf ball, as does the game of golf. There the resemblance seems to end, however, and it is not hard to make the case that far from being part of the game, putting is a weird mutational offspring whose chief function is to haunt accomplished golfers. It seems more like a contradiction of golf than a part of it. Harold Hilton, the only amateur to win the British Open Championship twice, put it with English reserve: "One often will find a man who has no idea of the game and how it should be played running in putts from all parts of the green, whilst, vice versa, players are to be found who though they have command of every stroke in the game, are often hopelessly at sea on the greens." Ben Hogan, whose problems with putting late in his career were well known, grumbled that golf should consist of players hitting their shots toward a stick on the green and then moving on to the next tee.

Golfers who are justly proud of their accomplishments on other parts of the course are almost embarrassed to admit success on the green. They act as if success compromises their inalienable rights as golfers to whine about the injustice of putting.

This antipathy for putting seems to rest on two facts: first, the extraordinary importance of putting, and second, not unrelated, its almost baffling complexity.

If it takes 72 strokes to tour a golf course in par, as it does on most courses, then precisely half those strokes are allotted for putts. No other type of stroke can be more than half as common.

Moreover, putts need to be more precise than woods or irons. They are the final strokes on a hole, and as such have the potential for redeeming bad shots or ruining good ones. Because there is likely to be greater equality among golfers off the tee and on the fairway than on the green, putting is often decisive, particularly in match play.

In the 1938 Professional Golfers' Association Championship, then a match-play tournament, Paul Runyan met Sam Snead in a scheduled 36-hole final round. On practically every hole, the younger and stronger Snead, with his marvelously graceful swing, outhit Runyan by fifty yards off the tee. But at the end, there was the diminutive Runyan, having putted brilliantly, an eight-and-seven winner.

With so much at stake on the green, it is not surprising that a cult of awe and mystery has enveloped putting, as if it were not complicated enough. Bending, squatting, kneeling, lying, muttering, writhing, or howling, golfers on the green look like some bizarre supplicants. Only the supernatural can help, they seem to be saying.

This discussion of putting offers no supernatural promise. It aims merely to present putting coherently, with the mumbo-jumbo, phony cures, and quack medicinemen excised if not exposed, and the accumulated wisdom, however insufficient, explained and investigated. You will not learn to putt by reading this chapter, but if the mysterious and nightmarish become more understandable, it might help you to stop worrying about your putting.

These claims are made in full realization that the putting bogeyman has proved hard to banish. Some of the best-intentioned, most compassionate attempts at reassurance for the putter have succeeded mainly in impeaching the credibility of

A matter of precision. Having only the slightest margin for error, golfers on the green become quite finicky. A few have charged that putting is all a nit-picking abomination of golf.

As a golfer ages, his putting tends to deteriorate before the other parts of his game. Opposite: *The elderly Sam Snead, eye riveted on the target, finds a modified croquet-mallet stance a steadying influence.* Above: *Arnold Palmer retains his knock-kneed stance but switches putters constantly.*

the expert. For example, a few years ago, when he was at the top of his game and, thus, considered the leading expert on everything from the flying shirt tail to the bogey grimace, Arnold Palmer opined, ". . . when our putting is sour . . . then we are in honest, interminable, miserable trouble." Arnie then carefully and at length demonstrated why and how such grief could be avoided. It was undeniably a matter of concentration and practice, he concluded, which everybody, large or small, young or old, should be able to learn. Presumably even Arnold Palmer in 1975, the year he putted so miserably that he changed putters close to a hundred times. The apostle of sweet reason (oh, how easy to be rational and charitable when the gods treat you that way) had become as voodooed as anyone else who ever swooned over a two-foot-long abomination of a golf shot.

Bernard Darwin, the late English golf writer, said of putting, "It is a strange thing that we know just how to do a thing at golf, and yet we cannot do it. . . . We are like men living on the brink of a volcano; we never know when and how suddenly destruction may overtake us. No precaution avails against Vesuvius."

And yet in contrast to this passive and pessimistic view, golfers who are putting well speak about "willing" the ball into the hole—a doctrine of almost religious determination and determinism. Johnny Miller has talked of virtually seeing the line of the putt before he strikes the ball. Bobby Jones wrote, ". . . I can truthfully say I have holed very few putts when I could not see definitely the path the ball should follow into the hole." Jack Nicklaus insisted that he knew a forty-foot putt would go in during the final round of the 1975 Masters (and it did, of course, for a birdie two on the sixteenth hole). "It becomes mind over matter," he says helpfully.

Obviously, putting is as much a mental as it is a physical exercise. However, this magical mystical experience is not wholly mysterious. The

If nothing else, putting elicits the feelings of a golfer. Clockwise from right: *Hope (David Hill), desolation (Tom Weiskopf), delight (Jane Blalock).*

168

psychology of putting is not simply a psych; it consists of some practical, if not always practicable, mechanics. So to begin this investigation of putting, we'll state that rational explanation can penetrate even the shrouded realm of the mind, wherein the fate of many a putt is determined.

The prime rule is to relax without losing concentration. "Putting is individual," says Nicklaus, "but there are certain fundamentals. To me one of them is comfort. I don't know of any good putters who aren't comfortable. And of course concentration." Once a golfer decides on a stance and stroke, his success rests on the mental process not only of analyzing the putt—reading the green, deciding the speed of the putt—but of staying free from tension or anxiety so as to be able to execute the stroke properly. Tension, or more precisely, apprehension, is disastrous.

To achieve this blissful state of composure, a routine appears to be helpful. Tom Weiskopf, one of the game's top players, was on a practice putting green at a tournament, trying to find the magic. Bert Yancey, another pro and Weiskopf's close friend, watched for a while, then remarked, "Your problem, Tom, is that you don't have a routine. One minute you take four looks at the hole, the next three. You have no system. Any time you deviate, you create tension."

Weiskopf dutifully developed a pattern. He took his stance, looked twice at the hole to gauge line and distance, then brought the clubhead back to strike the ball. His putting improved.

Years earlier, Arthur D'Arcy ("Bobby") Locke of South Africa created his own system, which he once described as a "drill." It never varied. He did his thinking before addressing the ball. Then he took two practice swings, stepped to the ball, looked once at the hole, and putted. Rule one: relaxation comes with regimen.

It is a bit like bowling or shooting foul shots. Spontaneously slinging the ball at the pins or the basket may work well at the start—better than the rank beginner expects—because the mind is at ease, allowing the body to function without hindrance. But at best—in the most sanguine persons—this is a hit-and-miss method. Those first spontaneous tries may look natural, even talented, but they are just educated guesses, no substitute for precise calculations. To succeed consistently, bowlers, foul shooters, golfers, and for that matter most athletes need a system that disposes of many of the variables without thought, and thereby allows a player to focus on a particular problem. A system that dispels distractions, that unclutters the mind, allows the putter to relax and to concentrate.

Concentration—every putter agrees that it is crucial but few can define it, or even understand precisely how it is attained. Most are satisfied simply to recognize it when it occurs—for example, during the 1920 British Women's Amateur on one of those linksland courses skirted by railroad tracks. Joyce Wethered, one of the better players in history, stood lining up a putt. At the instant she began the stroke, a whistle from a passing locomotive blew. Wethered never flinched, and the ball rolled into the cup. Asked later if she had been disturbed by the whistle from the locomotive, Wethered responded, "What whistle?"

It was a good indication that Billy Casper had lost his concentration when, several years ago during the final round of the Los Angeles Open, Casper complained that he was disturbed by the indiscriminate clicks of spectators' cameras during his backswing. Casper bogeyed the last hole and lost a sudden-death playoff to Bob Lunn.

"You must be able to concentrate," says Casper, usually an excellent putter. "It's a very big factor. But not the only one. I think feel and touch are very important in putting. Some individuals are gifted with these, but you have to work hard, too. Putting is as much practice as it is natural ability."

Apparently, concentration, feeling, and touch go together. The practice that Casper says is

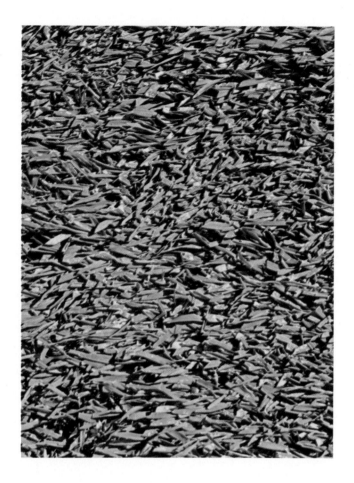

necessary to develop feeling and touch may basically be practice to *concentrate* on feeling and touch. As a young man, Casper used to practice putting in the dark so as to help him concentrate on the feeling of the stroke.

Bobby Jones also practiced putting after dark and recorded some revealing observations about the experience. "I used to go over to the club and putt with a friend and neighbor on the practice green near the tenth tee. The moonlight revealed the hole, and it also made visible the more prominent slopes and undulations, but it left kindly obscured the more subtle slopes and irregularities. In this revealing light, it was a source of wonderment to my friend and me that we invariably putted better than in broad daylight,

especially when it came to holing out from distances of up to eight or ten feet."

For both Casper and Jones, a little adversity (darkness) helped the putter concentrate on the essentials, be it the feel or the line of the putt.

Tony Jacklin could even turn the adversity of a pressure situation to his advantage. He once said, "If I walk up to a three-foot putt and start thinking of the consequences of the putt, what it means if I miss it or make it, how I missed the same putt the day before, then I'm not concentrating. When you are concentrating, you're thinking only of making the putt and not about anything outside that." Jacklin had the happy faculty of using the importance of a putt to force him to concentrate on the putt itself.

The surface of the green appears to be as uniformly nonresistant as a pool table, above right, *but it is in fact distinctly grained,* above. *The problem of slope also requires meticulous attention,* opposite.

One putt by Jacklin remains lodged in the memory. It came at the ninth hole of the final round of the 1970 U.S. Open. Dave Hill was closing in on Jacklin when Tony knocked a putt so hard that the ball struck the back of the hole and bounced into the air before dropping in. From there, Jacklin moved inexorably toward the championship that made him the first Briton in half a century to win the U.S. Open.

Such confidence and the concentration that inspires it is an uncommon gift. Concentration is not easy and the pressure of putting usually makes it only more difficult. Because putting is so important, it is only natural to be distracted into worrying about the consequences rather than the execution of the putt. Before long the putter finds himself not trying to make the putt but only to avoid missing it—fatal, self-fulfilling apprehension.

There is the old story, told by Bernard Darwin, of David Grant, a fine golfer, "turning round on someone who was knocking them in the hole from all parts of the green." Said Grant, " 'If ye had tae keep a wife an' six bairns ye widna put like that.' "

Then there is the famous occupational malady known as "the yips" (Tommy Armour's apt description). The golfer stands over a relatively short putt and freezes. When he finally can activate the putter, it leaps forward as if it were released from a slingshot, with predictably wild results. Ben Hogan, the most famous victim of the disease, felt it most acutely in the 1954 Masters, when he three-putted the thirteenth hole, four-putted the fifteenth, and three-putted the seventeenth. When on the eighteenth he needed to sink a six-footer to win, he stood off the green and reportedly made more than a hundred practice strokes, all different. Not surprisingly he missed the putt, dropped into a tie (with Sam Snead) and lost the playoff.

Part of it is physical—nothing more complex than the deterioration process called aging. Older golfers, after years of performing those delicate operations on the green, can lose the feel in the muscles that control the putter. But mostly the yips is a disease of the nerves. When a person gets nervous, his hands may tremble because they contain small muscles, which are more susceptible to tension.

A cure for the yips? Alex Smith, an old Scottish pro, went so far as to advise, "If you're going to miss 'em, miss 'em quick," on the theory that the longer one stands over a putt the more likely one will be to tremble over it. Fair enough, but the cure Smith suggested may be only another form of the disease—failure to concentrate. The fellow who quick-hits his putts in order to avoid stewing over them is likely also to avoid concentrating on them.

No, it's not so much how long you take to putt, but what you do with the time. Jack Nicklaus: "People say I stand over a putt for a long time before I make the stroke, but it doesn't seem that long to me. I'm waiting for a feeling that I can make the stroke I want. Very definitely putting is mostly in your head."

Enter the magic word—confidence. Continues Nicklaus, "Very often you get the confidence that you can make every putt. When you feel you can make every one, you don't have any apprehension about your stroke." Confidence cannot be said to be a cure for apprehension; it is the sign of its absence, a natural corollary to concentration. In truth there is no cure for apprehension to be found without delving into the troubled psyche of the putter whose deep-seated fears cause him to lose all concentration and to tremble over seemingly innocuous two-footers. Disciplining and ordering his movements on the green will help him to concentrate but not force him to; they will not necessarily inure him to the pressures of putting.

At this point the best we can offer, in lieu of psychoanalysis, is what we hope is a little soothing fatalism. There is a lot of simple chance involved in putting, and anyone suffering from the trauma of doubts about his technique would do well to

Ben Hogan was the most famous casualty of putting jitters, termed "the yips." Here he has just sunk one but seems more grimly satisfied than pleased.

remember that at least part of his inadequacy can be laid to simple bad luck. When you are aiming at a target only slightly larger than a teacup (4.25 inches in diameter, to be exact), it takes only a fraction of an inch to foil the shot. Luck is more than capable of exceeding that margin of error. Of course sometimes luck will salvage a mis-hit ball. But the point is that no one can fully control the exacting discipline of putting, and those who recognize that fact are more likely to survive its inevitable disappointments. Says Casper matter-of-factly, "There are times when you can hit the ball well, so solidly, right on the line, and it just doesn't go in. Other days, you don't make solid contact but the ball just runs into the hole. You just have to be in position all the time to try to make the putt." In other words, treat every putt as makable, but don't be deluded into believing your best efforts can overcome invisible bumps or pebbles or some other devilish imperfections on

God's most finely manicured green earth.

Putt comes from the word, "put." The golfer puts, or places, the ball (1.68 inches in diameter) into the cup set in the ground. He uses a relatively short club, its clubface virtually perpendicular to the ground.

Unlike shots that require a full swing, there is no specific method of putting. Some golfers spread their feet more than a yard apart. Others keep their feet pinned together. Some stand upright; some crouch so low they might be searching for four-leaf clovers. Ken Myers, an amateur from Portland, Oregon, putts by holding the putter behind his back and swinging it between his legs. He claims this style stiffens the legs, stabilizes the arms, and looks much less ridiculous than missing an 18-inch putt with a conventional style. (Not that he makes all of them with this style.)

If they have nothing else in common in the way they stand, most putters do favor immobility. The body must not move once the stroke is begun. The slightest turn of the head or wrist is enough to throw off the putt. Many golfers use a slightly knock-kneed or pigeon-toed alignment to achieve stability. Arnold Palmer in the early 1960s was the archetype—his knees almost touching, his head and body rigid, and, not incidentally, his putts dropping from hither and yon.

Some putters, like Myers, go so far as to all but freeze even the arms and allow the club to swing like a pendulum. Sam Snead, faced with a case of the yips in his later years, adopted the croquet method, by which he stood directly behind the ball and swung the putter between his legs. When in 1968 the croquet method was outlawed, Snead modified his stance so that now he stands next to the ball, as required, but faces directly toward the cup with the side of his right foot next to the ball. He grips the top of the putter with his left hand and the middle of the shaft with his right, the latter hand providing impetus and guidance for the

175

*Better to be fatalistic than superstitious about near misses,
but when a ball hovers over the cup in seeming defiance of the laws
of gravity, incredulity is in order. Ben Crenshaw is the victim.*

pendulum stroke. "It's great for old folks and golfers with bad nerves," Sam says of this "sidesaddle" method.

Peter Trevillion, author of the humbly titled book, *The Perfect Putting Method*, advises a standard stance—side of the left foot facing the cup, for a right-handed golfer. But like Snead, he clutches the top of the grip in his left hand and uses the putter like a pendulum. His right hand holds the club far down the shaft—only eight inches from the blade for short putts. By this method, he says, he shifts the burden of the stroke from the small, tension-susceptible muscles of the

hands to the larger, more stable muscles of the arms. He claims never to miss a putt of less than four feet.

But the consensus seems to be that the hands, or at least the wrists, should do at least some of the work, perhaps precisely because they are more sensitive. Palmer and Casper are wrist putters. Johnny Miller and Nicklaus use a combination of arms and hands to deliver the stroke. The issue apparently comes down to how much the golfer should "feel" the ball. The pendulum stroke, as mechanical and invariable as possible, seems to keep feel to a minimum, as if

Whether hunched (John Brodie, above left), or erect (Judy Rankin, above), golfers strive for immobility in their stances. Opposite: The back, black profile of Gary Player makes the point dramatically.

once the golfer has decided how much force and what direction to give his putt, he needs only a machinelike stroke to transform this information into an accurate stroke. The golfer activates the putter more than he directs it. Follow-through is minimal.

There is some evidence that a mechanical method becomes less effective at slightly greater distances. Over the years tests have been performed with a machine that produces a perfectly smooth stroke. Yet even the machine made only six of ten attempts from ten feet.

Members of the wrist school and the hand-arm adherents, on the other hand, emphasize a longer, more sweeping stroke, as if the golfer is guiding the ball as well as tapping it. The objective seems to be to follow the line of the putt from in back of the ball through the ball, fusing the path of the putter with that of the ball. Says Nicklaus, "You [should] have your eyes over the line of the putt, over the target line or an extension through it, and . . . try to keep your hands moving through the stroke."

This style can lead to less uniform strokes than the croquet approach produces, and Nicklaus, for one, seems to prefer it that way. "During a tournament, I might use eighteen different strokes," he says. "I may take the putter straight back and straight through. Sometimes I take it inside. Sometimes I hit down on the ball, sometimes up, sometimes hook. Sometimes I cut it. I do a lot of different things when I putt."

Though such sophisticated variations are not recommended for the poor novice who has all he can do to master a basic stroke, the principle is worth noting—flexibility. Putts, like any other golf shots, are not all the same, and to be a brilliant putter you must be able to tailor your stroke to suit the putt. At this point putting becomes more of an art than a science. You can calculate only so much; sooner or later you will have to guess (the scientist might call it hypothesize, the artist intuit)

Arnold Palmer has always used as rigid a stance as anyone. These days, however, the putts are no longer dropping. Clearly, one's stance can encourage but not ensure control.

as to just what a particular stroke should look like. Putting is often a creative process.

Back to basics; you can't play symphonies until you master scales. One principle easy enough to grasp is the grip. Most pros, assuming that they putt from the standard stance, use the reverse overlap grip—(for a right-hander) the forefinger of the left hand over the knuckles of the right. This grip prevents the right hand from "taking control," that is, jerking, the putter during the stroke.

In general the hands and arms ought to join into one smoothly functioning unit. Bobby Jones found that by bending over far enough to create a bend in his left elbow he attained the desired equilibrium. He confessed, "Although I should, by now, have learned how deceitful are the gods of golf, I could not resist the temptation to write that this [crouch and consequent left-elbow bend] comes very close to being a panacea for all putting ailments."

Everyone agrees that the delivery of the stroke should be smooth and that a happy marriage between the two hands facilitates the process. The sticking point appears to be the fingers or wrists, the snap of which powers the ball. It is simply not a naturally smooth motion, whether or not the hands are working in conjunction. To control this movement, Casper emphasizes keeping the blade of the putter close to the ground, apparently a means to put somewhat more left wrist or arm in the stroke. Walter Travis, one of the top players and putters just after the turn of the century, used a mental aid. He said he liked to visualize the stroke as an attempt to drive an imaginary tack into the ball.

Bobby Locke judged the quality of his putts by sound as well as by sight. If the clubface striking the ball produced a "ping," the putt had been well struck. A dull, non-resonating sound signaled a poor stroke.

According to Locke and many others, an essential characteristic of a well-struck putt is topspin. "The ball rolling end over end, if not going too fast, will fall in from the side of the cup," he observed. Locke also claimed that the player who "consistently can produce such a roll usually develops the best sense of distance." Which brings us to gauging how hard to strike the putt.

"Never up, never in," advises one old golf motto, which is often taken to mean that a putt must be struck hard enough to roll past the cup if it is to have any chance of going in. Many golfers, including Nicklaus and Frank Beard, disagree and attempt to define with their putts the level of force just over the minimum necessary for the ball to reach the hole. They point out that a slowly rolling ball not precisely on target stands a better chance of dropping into the cup than an identically aimed "charged" shot. "When you play fast greens," says Nicklaus, "you'd better learn to die [terminate] the ball at the hole, or you're going to miss a lot of putts. . . . That's one reason I don't putt well on slow greens; you have to charge the ball, and I don't putt that way."

What is a fast green? A slow green? Grass is grass, isn't it? To a point. There are two species of turf grass used for putting greens in the United States: Bermuda grass and bent grass. Bermuda is a wiry grass, grown mostly in the humid, warm regions of the country, particularly the Southeast. It can be distinguished by its horizontal growth; at first glance it looks like a fresh crewcut. Bent is commonly grown in the country's cooler locales. and it is softer than Bermuda. Bent grows vertically first, then flattens out. It is faster than Bermuda because the flat surface restricts the roll of the ball less than the thatching of Bermuda, which grabs the ball slightly.

Bermuda greens are more consistent than bent greens. On the slippery surface of bent, the ball is played further back in the stance—slightly more toward the rear foot—than it is in Bermuda grass, and given less of a "slap" with the putter, which results in less topspin.

A glimpse of the Nicklaus routine—above right: appraising the situation; opposite: flicking away an imaginary obstacle . . .

The more a green is watered, the softer and slower it becomes. The more a green is mowed, the shorter and faster it becomes. The fastest greens, then, would consist of closely cut, dry bent grass; the slowest, long wet Bermuda.

The speed of the green is determined in addition by the grain of the grass, that is, the direction in which the grass grows. Grain is most easily ascertained by looking at the grass between the ball and the hole. If the grass appears shiny or glossy, then the grain runs away from you; if it appears dull, then the grain runs toward you. The difference can be significant. Down grain, you would try to hit a 25-foot putt with the power of a 20-footer on a green with negligible grain. Into the grain, you would try to stroke the ball as if the putt were 30 feet with no grain. Obviously, the failure to study the grain will leave a second putt that is, in the phrase of British golf announcer and writer Henry Longhurst, "eminently missable."

Sidehill grain in either direction can be determined by studying the cup. If the grass around three-quarters of the cup is closely trimmed and the grass around the remaining one-quarter is ragged and inconsistent, the grain runs from the ragged edge—which has been bent but not cut by the mowers—toward the closely trimmed portion.

Bent grass grows away from mountains and toward water, which brings us to the question of break, or slope, in a green. It is said that greens always break toward water—a handy insight unless you happen to be on the sixteenth green at Cypress Point (all but surrounded by the Pacific Ocean) or at Augusta National (several hundred miles inland). A more accurate means of determining the direction and degree of break is to crouch behind the ball. (A few zealots have even been known to lie on the green.) Or the golfer can use the so-called "plumb bob" system—holding the putter loosely by the handle and allowing the head to determine a vertical line.

By looking with one eye, then the other, the golfer can calculate the slope.

Newer courses, those built since World War II by such architects as Robert Trent Jones, have large greens with severe but obvious breaks. The greens of half-century-old courses have more subtle rolls that are often more difficult to decipher. In the 1970 British Open at St. Andrews, Doug Sanders stood on the eighteenth green looking over what he took to be a simple straight four-footer. It turned out, however, to break slightly to the left, causing Sanders's ball to slide just past on the left. The extra stroke dropped Sanders into a tie for first with Jack Nicklaus, who won the playoff the next day.

On putts of a foot or two with little obvious slope, the golfer does best to aim at the center of the cup, or at least not outside the edge, the break being negligible at that short a distance. On long putts with clear breaks, most golfers aim at a spot on the green between the cup and the ball. When the degree of break is unclear, it's safest to allow oneself margin for error on the high side of the hole, because once the ball breaks below the hole there is no chance that it can curl in. A charging putt can be hit straighter than a dying one because the pull of the slope affects the ball more as it slows down.

There was a time when a golfer needn't have learned all these lessons in agronomy before becoming a competent putter. On many courses the greens consisted of sand. And even today in places where grass is sparse or nonexistent—the Middle East, Alaska—sand or oiled sand is used for greens, or should that be browns? After each putt, the sand surface is smoothed, or dragged, so that it remains true, truer than grass.

Mavens of this cruel pastime may have noticed by now that this discussion of putting has so far all but ignored the instrument with which that task is accomplished—the putter. The oversight has been

. . . opposite: *tending to the stroke ("I wait for a feeling that I can make the stroke I want");* right: *the confidence of success.*

deliberate—an attempt to consign the hysteria over putters to the fringe of the discussion, where it belongs. What wisdom has been unearthed in the obsessive pursuit of the perfect putter is probably best encapsulated by the terse advice of George Low, a jowly sort who may have been the best putter in the history of golf. Said Low, ''If you've got a putter you can use, hang on to it. I don't care what it looks like.''

Apparently no one is listening. The history of putting is in large part the succession of fads in putters, and it's getting worse. Early in this century there were basically only two types of putting clubs—the deep-bladed ''Calamity Jane'' putter, used so successfully by Bobby Jones, and the

plain mallet. In the 1950s, a gentleman named John Reuter introduced a shallow, center-shafted blade with the dramatic name ''Bull's Eye.'' Golfers switched to it en masse. Jack Nicklaus created a stir when he won the 1967 U.S. Open with a putter called ''White Fang.'' In fact, Nicklaus's White Fang was nothing but a Bull's Eye putter that his wife had painted white. No matter. Golf shops across the country were swamped with demands for paint jobs on their Bull's Eye putters. Fortunately, Nicklaus switched back to his old-style putter, White Fang died a fast death, and pro shops put away their paint brushes.

Then a former engineer for General Electric, Karsten Solheim, came up with a cross between a

Opposite: *Grip grist—Johnny Miller, Jane Blalock, and Jack Nicklaus, left to right, all overlap the knuckles of the right hand with the forefinger of the left to prevent the right hand from controlling the stroke. Below: Hubert Green demonstrates the plumb bob method of lining up a putt.*

The long and the short of it. Above: On short putts there is no need to take into account the slope of the green and the grain of the grass. Just put the ball in the center of the hole. Left: On longer putts, overestimate rather than underestimate the break.

189

mallet and a blade that, because of the sound emitted when it struck the ball, he called the "Ping." (So much for Bobby Locke.) That was the rage of the late 1960s. In the mid-1970s, another amateur experimenter, Dave Taylor of Carmel, California, created a mallet putter with broad black and gray sight lines across the top that caused it to be called "Zebra." In early 1976, Ray Floyd won the Masters with a Zebra and the next week Don January won the MONY (Mutual of New York) Tournament of Champions with one. Magic? Not quite. A few weeks earlier Hubie Green had won three straight tournaments with a blade putter manufactured by the Great Lakes Company—a firm that had gone out of business in 1931.

There is a lesson in this fuss over putters, beyond the obvious one that the person is more important than the club. Putting is not only a difficult skill to master; it is a psychological trap. Whether or not you do it well, it seems to cheapen the value of the more classic strokes, hence the discomfort of the pros when they're putting well, their agony when they're putting poorly. You're a bad putter: too bad. You're a good one: so what? Whatever you gain in composure pales in the face of resentment from other golfers. So it is no wonder that the golfer is looking for an easy way out. The ideal putting club, if it could be found, would be not so much a miracle cure as a sedative. It wouldn't make putting pleasurable, only painless. That is the best that can be hoped for from this trying exercise.

Modest attempts to help reach the goal of less painful putting have been frowned upon by the ruling bodies of golf (who might have been expected to look more leniently on honest efforts to master the skill). When, in 1904, Walter Travis putted brilliantly in becoming the first foreigner to win the British Amateur, the Royal and Ancient Golf Association of St. Andrews, ruling body of British golf, banned the use of his type of club, a mallethead with a center shaft. It took half a century before the association realized Travis hadn't blasphemed against the sacred ritual of putting.

More recently, touring pro Dave Hill had the bright idea of having his caddie crouch down immediately behind the blade of the putter as Hill made the stroke. In time other golfers, Johnny Miller, for one, adopted the practice. Hill said he wanted his caddie to determine if the stroke was true. Miller liked the idea because it prevented him from seeing, and hence being distracted by, anything behind his line. But the United States Golf Association, the nation's ruling body, outlawed the practice at the start of the 1976 season. The USGA held that such help from the caddie was unfair. Moreover, some purists argued that the arrangement looked uncomely!

Somebody, it seems, has a stake in keeping this game within a game as trying as possible. Why? Is the challenge of golf somehow insufficient without the injustices of putting tacked on? Obviously, that's a loaded question. Perhaps it can best be answered by what wise golfers (and nongolfers) have recognized for a long time: golf wasn't meant to be fair. Once that is understood, then everything in the game, particularly putting, becomes, if not easier, then less irritating.

A golf course is really an obstacle course, and the greens, as the most exacting, treacherous, and capricious obstacles of all, are the climactic challenges. You succeed not so much by getting hot as by keeping your cool—never conquering, only coping. Putting is very much part of the game after all.

A caddie helps and, in this case, seems
even more intent than the golfer, Ai-Yu Tu.

6
Lyrical Golf
A Photographic Essay

Look for the character of this game in the interludes, for in no other sport are they as dominant. They dwarf the action as the course dwarfs the player.

Tony Jacklin

Sandra Post

Johnny Miller

Kathy Whitworth

Partly it is a waiting game. When there is nothing to do, the moods are subtle but revealing. When the thinking starts, a cloak of concentration prevails.

Tom Weiskopf

Bruce Crampton

A golf shot doesn't just happen; it is prepared. Yet the spontaneous splashes of color and strange twists of shape on a course suggest that shotmaking can never be precise.

Tom Watson

Ray Floyd

The action, when it finally comes, shatters not only the easy rhythms preceding it but the tableau surrounding it. Examine the scene of the shot and you will find a discordant slice of motion; all else is still.

Mike Morley

Hubert Green

Miller Barber

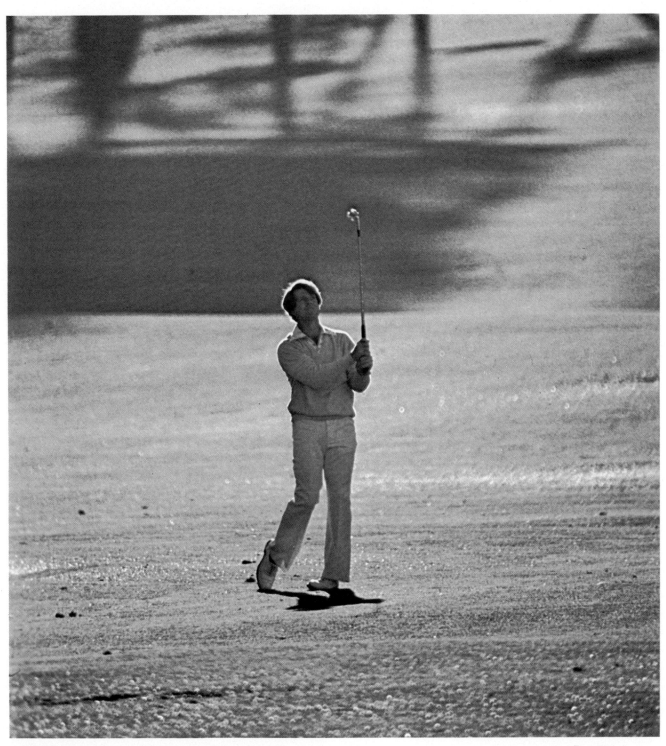

Tom Watson

A golfer controls the swing and through it the shot, but it is the target that gives meaning to his efforts and, sometimes, seems to exert a control of its own.

Lionel Hebert

Buddy Allin

Carol Mann

Waiting, again, this time for the verdict. The most suspenseful moments in golf come in those few seconds when a player anticipates what is now all but inevitable but not yet quite clear.

Lee Trevino

Jack Nicklaus

Arnold Palmer

JoAnne Carner

**In the end there may be roaring delight or stinging
disappointment, radiant triumph or rueful disgust.
Such powerful feelings overflow the present and shape
the future of a round, the nature of which will be
revealed in subsequent interludes.**

7
The Ultimate Grand Slam
A Fan's Fantasy Tournament

"We fed a formidable mass of information to a Bowmar Brain and in short order had our field of sixteen. Here they are. . . . Quite a field, and of course a blockbuster of a package for the television people and Madison Avenue guys. . . ."

We will call it the World Classic Invitational. It will be the sixteen greats of all time paired off in head-to-head combat, a match-play contest that will, finally, answer: Who is the greatest golfer in history?

As you can see, the World Classic (or the WCI, as we shall call it) is not going to be another of those Bing Hope Eastern Delta United Celebrity Charity Opens that they play every week from January to December on golf courses that ought to be parking lots. This has to be the greatest golf tournament ever. And that requires rather extraordinary arrangements.

Obviously, the WCI is too big for any one course or complex of courses. So we will play each round on a different golf course—not Latrobe or any other Palmer course, not Muirfield Village, Hilton Head, or any other Nicklaus course. We'll play the first match in California, out at Pebble Beach, on the Monterey Peninsula, overlooking Carmel Bay. The eight winners at Pebble will journey across the country and then the Atlantic for the quarterfinals at the Old Course at St. Andrews in Scotland. (The eight losers at Pebble Beach automatically lose all their endorsement contracts, become 10-handicappers at the Dyker Beach muny outside Brooklyn, and forfeit forever the right to call everyone else "pards.") The four survivors at St. Andrews will return to North America and meet in Pittsburgh for the 36-hole semifinals at Oakmont. And for the grand finale, the winners at Oakmont will square off over 36 holes at the Merion Golf Club on Philadelphia's Main Line.

As for the selection of the contestants, the sixteen greatest golfers ever, we'll have to decide on some ground rules. If, for example, Arnold Palmer makes the Select Sixteen, do we get the Palmer who hitches his pants and makes 20-foot birdie putts at the same time, or do we get the Palmer who changes his tinted Elton John specs during his backstroke but still cannot drop a six-inch, straight-in putt for a triple bogey? And, on a somewhat less substantive question, will we have the Jack Nicklaus who was so portly that they used to call him "Blob-O," "Ohio Fats," "Whaleman," and "Fat Jack," or will we have the Nicklaus who got slim, discovered the Hollywood fluff-dry hair style, ordered some clothes that fit, became an instant matinee idol, won a couple of million dollars, and turned 30 years old, all on the same day, it seemed? To resolve this delicate matter, we polled every U.S. Golf Association (USGA), Royal and Ancient (R&A), and Professional Golfers' Association (PGA) official worth his blazer, striped tie, red armband, and collapsible seat, and requested permission to have each player considered as he was (or is) at the prime of his career. The vote from this crusty panel was extremely close, but in the end the motion carried, and we were free to choose among such luminaries as the turn-of-the-century Harry Vardon, who won three British Opens in four seasons, the Grand Slam Bobby Jones of 1930, the Palmer who could putt without granny glasses, and the sleek, if not skinny, Nicklaus.

Then we collected all the history books, rule books, memos, and assorted information from the USGA, the R&A, and the PGA; the notebooks of Joe Dey, Herbert Warren Wind, Dan Jenkins, Angelo Argea, Mark McCormack, Frank Pasquale, Roone Arledge, Robert Trent Jones, and Jane Blalock; the bound volumes of *Sports Illustrated, Golf, Golf Digest,* the *USGA Journal,* and *Palm Springs Life*; and, finally, simply all the books ever written about golf, including *Peeling Potatoes at Ft. Sill Taught Me How to Win the U.S. Open*, by Sgt. Orville Moody, U.S. Army, with George Plimpton. We fed this formidable mass of information to a Bowmar Brain and in short order had our field of sixteen. Here they are, in the order the computer dispatched them: Dr. Cary Middlecoff. Arnold Palmer. Harry Vardon. Gary Player. Walter Hagen. Lee Trevino. Gene Sarazen.

Jack Nicklaus. Sam Snead. Byron Nelson. Julius Boros. Peter Thomson. Ben Hogan. Bobby Jones. Johnny Mixxxxx. Correction. Tom Weisxxxxxx. Correction. Billy Casper.

No Johnny Miller? Sorry. Miller has won only two major championships, just one more than the aforementioned Sergeant Moody, who is not on the selection list even as an alternate. Tom Weiskopf? With all his unlimited potential, Tom has also won just one major championship, the British Open Championship in 1973.

Let's examine the playing credentials of our sixteen. Among them they have won the staggering total of 34 British Opens, 27 United States Opens, 21 PGA crowns, and 21 green coats at the Masters. Vardon, for example, won six British Opens. Hogan and Jones both won the U.S. Open four times. Nicklaus has taken five Masters; Hagen, not Hogan, won the PGA five times when that tournament was conducted at match play.

Quite a field, and of course a blockbuster of a package for the television people and Madison Avenue guys. Without their Yankee imperialistic whipout this ultimate golf tournament might have to rely on New York City municipal bonds or plastic magic for a purse. No way. Cold cash.

ABC offered to buy North American television rights for $7.5 million plus two autographed copies of Howard Cosell's latest autobiography. NBC studied the bid and decided it needed to go only a penny higher if it excluded the Cosell books. At this point Ben Hogan discerned a conflict of interest if ABC got the package, since Byron Nelson still works for the network as an analyst on its golf telecasts. Hogan observed, "Byron would probably have ABC do slow-motion instant replays of all his shots instead of covering our matches." Nicklaus thought NBC suspect because it had bought Palmer's company for $15 million. So by process of elimination the rights went to CBS (which had come in with the best offer of $7.5 million and two cents anyway), provided that the

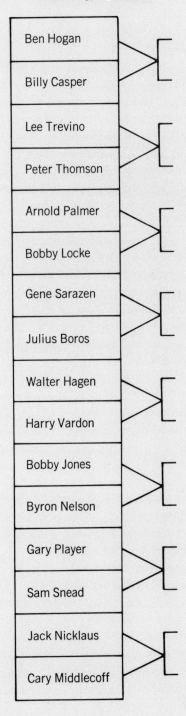

**First Round—Pebble Beach
Monterey, California**

Ben Hogan
Billy Casper

Lee Trevino
Peter Thomson

Arnold Palmer
Bobby Locke

Gene Sarazen
Julius Boros

Walter Hagen
Harry Vardon

Bobby Jones
Byron Nelson

Gary Player
Sam Snead

Jack Nicklaus
Cary Middlecoff

network agreed not to use retired NFL quarterbacks as play-by-play announcers on the eighteenth green.

Unfortunately, CBS had some other ideas. "We want to do something innovative," A. Q. Phelps Somebody told us. "We'd like to put a remote camera inside one of Nicklaus's golf balls to record the exact moment of impact of a tee shot. We want to use the cockpit of the airborne Goodyear Blimp as the first tee at Pebble. That would give us a long downhill shot to a bip of grass. The fairways would be dyed blue and the players would use red golf balls. Imagine the spectacular effects on the home screen."

Tactfully, we explained to CBS that we envisioned a more subdued presence for television at the greatest tournament of all time. "The only thing you guys don't want to do," we said, risking humor, "is sell the ball-washing concession to one of the soap companies." Nobody laughed. "Geez," marveled one dreamy-eyed exec, "that's a helluva idea." Quickly we changed the subject and, playing it straight the rest of the way, concluded the negotiations. Each player would be guaranteed $50,000 just for showing up at Pebble for the first round. First-round winners would collect another $50,000; second-round winners $100,000; semifinal winners $150,000; and the grand champ a grand million. Thus, the big winner would gross $1.35 million.

"We'll pay all the travel expenses," we informed our players grandly. "All you need to do is sign your John Hancock at the hotels, clubhouses, and selected taverns. Any questions?"

Lee Trevino piped up. "Who's John Hancock?"

Finally it was time for the draw. Ben Hogan provided the white cap, and we had a blindfolded accountant from Price, Waterhouse drop in 16 three-by-five cards, each with the name of one of our Select Sixteen. Lawrence Welk drew out the names, and Dom Mirandi, the official scorer of the PGA, was there to scribble them on an Acushnet

draw sheet. Bantam Ben Hogan came up first. Then Welk picked out Casper's card. So our first match would be Hogan against Casper, and someone joked, "Casper will need more than the Mormon Tabernacle Choir to beat Ol' Bantam." As the draw progressed we came up with the following matches, in order: Trevino vs. Thomson, Palmer vs. Locke, Sarazen vs. Boros, Hagen vs. Vardon, Jones vs. Nelson, Nicklaus vs. Middlecoff, and Player vs. Snead.

"All right, gentlemen," we said. "We'll see all of you at the Del Monte Lodge two weeks from Friday."

Despite all its natural beauty and splendor there

We'll play our first round at Pebble Beach and, in order not to increase the challenge of the course at the expense of its charm, order a brisk but manageable breeze.

Like all great golf courses, Pebble Beach demands a little bit of everything from shotmakers. Though not without challenge, the first five holes lull the golfer into a false sense of security because the next thirteen are often brutal. The seventh, eighth, ninth, and tenth holes stretch along Carmel Bay and feel the full force of the often ferocious wind. The seventh hole, for instance, is supposed to be a simple par three—a little wedge shot over the bush to a tiny green sitting on some rock at the edge of the ocean. On the adjacent beach there is enough sand to stock a desert, and a lot of bleached-blond beach boys hanging ten in the surf caps. One or two days a year it *is* just a simple shot; the rest of the season, though, the shot might call for anything from a four-wood to a five-iron, aimed, as the caddies like to say, "for downtown Honolulu, thirty-five hundred miles off to the right." The eighth, ninth, and tenth holes are monster par fours that require long, precise tee shots and accurate long iron or wood approaches to well-trapped greens perched atop the oceanside cliffs. At the eighth, the long approach must travel over an ocean chasm; at the ninth and tenth, the greens tilt sharply to the right. Tommy Bolt—Terrible Tempered Tommy—double-bogeyed the eighth and ninth holes during the Crosby one year, then told Bing himself, "I'm going to put a forty-five revolver to your head and make you play the eighth and ninth holes until you par them."

Pebble Beach then wanders back through the woods and disturbs the deer for a few holes before returning for the oceanside killers: the par-three seventeenth, some 225 yards into the wind to an artfully bunkered humpbacked green with the ocean yawning behind it, and finally, the greatest finishing hole in all golf—the par-five, interminable eighteenth that runs along the ocean on a jagged cliff. Hook a shot on the eighteenth at Pebble Beach and, well, your ball might wash up in Adelaide, Australia, some century. All in all, eight

above the Pacific on some cliffs overlooking Carmel Bay, Pebble Beach can be an ugly place to play golf. The players on the regular pro tour bravely risk their health and sanity every January when they stop at Pebble for the Bing Crosby Pro-Am Tournament. Smorgasbord golf, the pros call Pebble Beach, for in one 18-hole trip around the old links they can play in desert heat, arctic cold, snow, sleet, hail, and hurricane winds, all in no particular order. Dan Jenkins once wrote that Pebble Beach is the world's leading argument for indoor golf. By scheduling our opening round for mid-June, though, we eliminated at least the snow from the list of possible hazards that would be confronting our Select Sixteen.

of the eighteen holes at Pebble Beach border the Pacific, moving Herbert Warren Wind to conclude that Pebble "undoubtedly occupies the most dramatic terrain of any course in the world."

Ironically, the weather at Pebble Beach for our opening round is serene by Pebble Beach standards. There is no snow but a rather stiff, unseasonably chilly breeze blowing off the Pacific. Sweater weather, the natives call it. Before the start of play, we assemble the Select Sixteen on the terrace of the Del Monte Lodge and serve them a buffet lunch; then, per Billy Casper's request, the Mormon Tabernacle Choir sings the national anthems of the United States, Great Britain, South Africa, and Australia—the four countries represented by the field. Lee Trevino jokingly

insists that we ought to play the Mexican National Anthem, too, but the choir does not know the words. When the music stops, we call on Archie Bunker to introduce the players to the fans around the terrace. (We had sold out all 30,000 tickets for the opening round in less time than it takes Nicklaus to read a two-foot putt.) As we secretly hoped he would, Bunker strays from our recommended script in his introduction. He calls Trevino "Old Taco Mouth"; suggests that Vardon ought to take his Vardon Grip and overlap it around his British neck; implies that Nicklaus has bleached his hair; announces that Hogan bought his white caps by the gross at a discount store in Nacogdoches, Texas; and, horrors, intimates that Palmer is a robot programmed and operated in

Opposite: *Others strolled; Bantam Ben Hogan stalked his way to victory.* Above left: *Billy Casper in trouble; he would be from the start against Hogan.* Above right: *Peter Thomson had a tightly controlled game that thrived on windy days—seemingly a natural for Pebble Beach.*

living color by Mark McCormack Productions on behalf of the National Broadcasting Company, Wake Forest, Learjet International Ltd., and Rolling Rock beer. So for the record, and to assuage any tender egos, here are the official introductions.

Ben Hogan. The Hawk, Bantam Ben, the man in the white cap. He caddied with Byron Nelson at Glen Gardens in Fort Worth. Taught Dan Jenkins how to hit a hook. Won the U.S. Open in 1948, 1950, 1951, and 1953; the Masters in 1951 and 1953; the PGA in 1946 and 1948; and the British Open in 1953—a total of nine major championships between 1948 and 1953. He was critically injured in a terrible automobile accident in February of 1949; then, in his first appearance back on the tour, tied Snead for first place in the 1950 Los Angeles Open. Nerves of steel, except on greens where he may "yip" an occasional short putt, and tremendous self-discipline. Occasionally, he hits a quick pull-hook that gallops forever. Known for his sarcasm. When Gary Player called and asked Hogan for some help with his game, Hogan asked Player whose clubs he used, and upon learning they were not Hogan clubs, he told Player to call the manufacturer for advice. Another time a young pro asked Hogan how he could become a better long putter. "Simple," Hogan said. "Hit your approach shots closer to the hole." Gary Player insists that Hogan is the best golfer he has ever seen. And who will ever forget the man's sensational 66, including a remarkable 30 on the back nine, at the Masters in 1967 when more than 20,000 teary-eyed people saluted his accomplishment as he limped up and down the fairways?

Billy Casper. Unfortunately he has always played in the shadows of the Big Three—Nicklaus, Palmer, and Player. Allergic to everything but money and religion. Devoted husband and father. Won the 1959 U.S. Open at Winged Foot with the greatest exhibition of putting ever seen and the 1966 Open at Olympic in San Francisco, catching

Opposite: *Lee Trevino came prepared for almost anything.* Above: *As always, the CO of Arnie's Army entertained the troops as he led them.*

Opposite: *Bobby Locke, putter discreetly but appropriately at his side.* Above left: *Gene Sarazen in 1932, the greatest year of his career. A quarter century later he was still going strong.* Left: *Julius Boros, not old before his time but great beyond his prime.*

Above: *Walter Hagen was America's first celebrity golfer; his game and personality demanded nothing less.* Opposite: *America remained a golfing colony of Britain until Harry Vardon, the last of the British golf monarchs, lost his crown.*

Palmer from seven shots back during the final nine holes and then beating him in an eighteen-hole playoff. Also won the Masters in 1970. Subsists on buffalo meat, fish, avocados, and pears. Absolute master of the short clubs, particularly the seven-iron, and the best in the game with a mallethead putter.

Peter Thomson. He hits the ball short and low and always on target. His game is perfectly suited for the wind, which helps account for his five victories in the British Open—1954, 1955, 1956, 1958, and 1965—and two second-place finishes. An Australian, he should feel right at home here at Pebble Beach, unless his opponent, Mr. Trevino, turns on the heat.

Lee Trevino. Lee was an obscure Texan-Mexican, or Mexican-Texan, until he finished in fifth place and won some $6,000 in the 1967 U.S. Open at Baltusrol. He used that money as a stake and ventured onto the pro tour. Since then Super Mex from El Paso has won two U.S. Opens—in 1968 at Oak Hill and in 1971 at Merion after a classic playoff duel with Jack Nicklaus; two British Opens—in 1971 and 1972; and a PGA championship in 1974, not to mention the hearts of golfers everywhere. His trademarks are the black cap with the sombrero emblem, the red shirt with the sombrero over the heart, and the taco. He learned how to handle pressure during his golf hustling days around Dallas. He says, "You don't know what real pressure is until you're playing a twenty-dollar Nassau and have only a dollar ninety-eight in your pocket." Nothing bothers him on the course, so don't be afraid to talk to him during play. He'll start talking if you don't.

Arnold Palmer. What can we say about Arnold Palmer that hasn't been said a million times before by Mark McCormack? Arnie's Army would have settled the Vietnam War in about half an hour. This man has won more than sixty championships, including the Masters in 1958, 1960, 1962, and 1964; the U.S. Open in 1960; and the British Open in

Bobby Jones, a golf scholar and gentleman, on the eve of his immortal Grand Slam. Never one to be intoxicated by success, he retired immediately after, and today history cannot imagine him at anything but his best.

1961 and 1962. About the only thing he has not won in golf is the PGA championship. He tinkers with golf clubs in the office complex next to his home. Has some three thousand clubs, most of which he has used at some point in his legendary career. Most of you people probably think that Arnold discovered golf and invented television; actually he brought golf to television and vice-versa with his gallery appeal. Always seems to be hitching his pants. Has lost three playoffs for the U.S. Open championship. A relentless rallying competitor, or as Gene Sarazen says, "Palmer's most dangerous when he's on the ropes, ready to be counted out."

Bobby Locke. For all of you who have putting problems—yes, even you, Arnold—we suggest that you talk to Bobby Locke. He is perhaps the greatest putter in the history of the game. He has used the same putter ever since his school days back in South Africa. Has won four British Opens —in 1949, 1950, 1952, and 1957—and has played extremely well in his forays to the United States.

Gene Sarazen. Let us return briefly to that great day at Augusta National, the final round of the 1935 Masters, and out on the par-five fifteenth hole Gene Sarazen is wondering how he can make up three shots on the leaders so late in a tournament. His drive was perfectly down the middle, as always. Then Gene struck what must rank as the greatest four-wood shot ever played. The ball carried the pond, landed on the fringe of the green, and rolled into the cup for an amazing double eagle two. Sarazen had made up his three-stroke deficit with a single shot, and naturally, he went on to win the championship. One of only four golfers who have won the big four —the U.S. and British Opens, the Masters, and the PGA—during his career. Popularized the sand wedge; in fact, some people insist that he invented the club. At the age of 56, he finished only 10 shots back of the champion in the 1958 British Open by shooting a remarkable even-par 288.

Julius Boros. Wake up, Julius Boros. Once Ol' Julius played 36 holes while Jack Nicklaus was addressing a tee shot. Don't blink when Julius approaches a shot or else you'll miss the shot. He doesn't take any practice swings or practice putts. And he is unflappable. Won the U.S. Open in 1952 at Dallas and then again in 1963 at Brookline when he was 43 years old. Won the PGA Championship in the San Antonio heat at the age of 48. And when today's round is over, Julius will probably go fishing. Toughest competition nowadays probably is his annual battle for the family championship with his gang of golfing sons.

Walter Hagen. In many ways the original Arnold Palmer. Sir Walter, they call him, or the Haig. He hits his share of bad shots, just like Arnold, but often charges back to win. Someone once said that Walter makes tying his shoelaces look more exciting than the other chap's hole-in-one. Has won the PGA championship five times, all at match play, two U.S. Opens, and four British Opens. Probably, he has won more tournaments with a hangover than almost anyone else with a clear head. He says, "I don't want to be a millionaire; I just want to live like one."

Harry Vardon. In case you people don't know it, the overlapping grip most of you use to grip the golf club is called the Vardon Grip, though Harry claims he didn't invent it, just popularized it. In any case, because of Vardon, nowadays golfers always make sure their V's point in the proper direction. Harry has never won a tournament here in North America, but back in England he has won six British Opens. Never displays so much as a sour look after one of his shots. A meticulous craftsman. The British claim that when Harry plays thirty-six holes the same day, the only hazards he meets on the second round are the divot marks he made on the first.

Bobby Jones. Let's not get into any prolonged intellectual discussions with Mr. Jones, boys, because we'll all be dormied at the turn. A graduate of Georgia Tech and Harvard Law School, he has a vocabulary greater than the rest of you combined. During the Roaring Twenties, as a lot of people like to call the Jones era, Bobby absolutely dominated this game. From 1921–30, he won five U.S. Opens and three British Opens, in addition to a slew of U.S. and British Amateur championships, but being a simon-pure amateur, Bobby collected only a lot of sterling silver trophies. Now has enough silver to open his own Tiffany's. In 1930, he won the Grand Slam (the Amateurs and the Opens of both the United States and Great Britain), promptly retired, and turned to the more serious pursuits of helping to organize and design the Augusta National club and later helping to establish the Masters tournament at Augusta.

Byron Nelson. Lord Byron. ABC's golfing colorman who pioneered the phrase "That's right, Chris." After picking up flaws in a swing on videotape replays, he likes to use a pointer to explain them. Master of the malaprop and other verbal goofs. ("Chris, the boys are hitting the ball longer now because they're getting more distance.") Won two PGAs, two Masters, and one U.S. Open. More important, won a record 11 straight PGA tournaments in 1945, starting with the Miami Four-Ball on March 11 and concluding with the Canadian Open on August 4. For those 11 victories he earned a total of $34,849.33, which is what the runner-up earns in some tournaments these days. Has a complicated swing, lacks confidence in his putting stroke, and still suffers from a growling stomach. Plays boldly but, strangely, despite his record, insists he does not have a killer instinct.

Jack Nicklaus. Only in his mid-thirties but in his fourteen years as a professional, Jack has won five Masters championships, four PGA championships, three U.S. Opens, two British Opens, four Australian Opens, four World Series of Golf championships, and a number of other tournaments, including the Ohio State Alumni Classic and the Lost Tree

Above right: *In 1945, the year Byron Nelson won 19 tournaments, he averaged a little more than 68 strokes per round. So much for those who say he was just lucky to have played against inferior, wartime competition. Opposite: Jack Nicklaus, the latest greatest, perhaps simply the greatest.*

Village Club Championship. All told, he has won more than sixty PGA-sponsored tournaments. Oh, yes. Also won a couple of U.S. Amateurs and a British Amateur in those days when he was not playing for dollars. Has won more than three million dollars. Deeply involved in golf course design these days, and his new course back in Columbus, Ohio—the little tester he calls the Memorial Course at Muirfield Village—may be the best course constructed in North America in decades. Here are a couple of eye-catchers: has missed the 36-hole cut only three times in the some one hundred and fifty tournaments he has entered so far in the 1970s; has finished second four times in the U.S. Open; has been voted PGA player-of-the-year four times; has won at least $100,000 on the tour in 13 of his 14 years as a pro. Bobby Jones put it quite succinctly: ''Nicklaus plays a game with which I am not familiar.''

Dr. Cary Middlecoff. Middlecoff the dentist. He doesn't hit his irons; he drills them. Won the U.S. Open in 1949, again in 1956, and the Masters in 1955. Every time he wins another tournament, he raises his dental rates. We only hope he fills cavities faster than he plays golf, because he is even slower than Nicklaus on the golf course, if that's at all possible.

Sam Snead. Born in 1912 but like Jack Benny insists he hasn't yet broken 40. Has won almost 100 PGA-sponsored tournaments, three Masters, a British Open, and more unfriendly Nassau challenges than you can count, but we're sure he'd trade them all for the only thing in golf that has eluded his grasp: the U.S. Open Championship. Learned to play this game by using a club made from a swamp-maple stick with a knot at one end, and may have the most natural swing of anyone. ''It's like swinging an ax,'' Sam once wrote. ''You don't jerk an ax back, and you don't give deep thought to swinging it down. The hands, arms, and feet all work by feel.'' Doesn't think he's a great putter, but Bantam once told him, ''Sam, you're the only person in the world who doesn't think you're a good putter!'' Fishes when he doesn't

Above left: *After Cary Middlecoff, center, won the Masters in 1955, President Eisenhower, right, debriefed him on it.* Above right *and* opposite: *A contrasting pair—Sam Snead, smooth even in the rough, and Gary Player, perpetually intense.*

play golf and likes to count his money when he isn't fishing or playing golf. Although too embarrassed to admit it, already has won about a half-dozen PGA and World Seniors championships.

Gary Player. Would someone please call down to the health spa and get Gary from the weight room? Mr. Muscles is a physical fitness nut from Johannesburg, South Africa. Never played golf until he was 15 years old, unlike, say, Jack Nicklaus, who used a seven-iron for a pacifier. Has won three British Opens, two PGAs, two Masters, and a U.S. Open, not to mention eight South African Opens, seven Australian Opens, five Piccadilly Match-Play championships and three World Series of Golf championships. Is the only foreign player ever to win the Masters. In 1965, he donated his entire $25,000 first-place winnings from the U.S. Open to American golf charities. Is a tenacious competitor; he has twice defeated Nicklaus in head-to-head matches over thirty-six holes, and once rallied from seven strokes down with seventeen holes to play and beat Tony Lema in England.

So, ladies and gentlemen, there you have them —our sixteen legends, the greatest players in the history of golf, the field for our WCl. Now, let's get on with our show.

For the most part, the first-round matches at Pebble Beach proved to be rather routine. Bantam Ben Hogan started the proceedings by beating Billy Casper 4-and-3, closing Casper with an eagle two at the fifteenth hole. Hogan missed only one fairway—the third, where he pull-hooked his drive into a ravine—and, surprise, clearly out-putted the usually meticulous Casper. Hogan rammed home birdie putts of 9 feet at the second hole, 13 feet at the fourth, 22 feet at the tenth, and 16 feet at the thirteenth. Then he holed out his pure seven-iron approach for the eagle at the fifteenth. Casper won only two holes—the third and the little

"... Walter Hagen somehow survived
half of Pebble Beach's bunkers, the
Pacific Ocean, three backyards, two
dirt roads, and a minor hangover
in edging Harry Vardon. . . ."

seventh—as he repeatedly caught the deep rough along the sides of the fairway with his drives and then encountered a balky putter on the greens. Lee Trevino promptly followed Hogan into the winner's circle with a 5-and-4 rout of Peter Thomson, who said afterward that Pebble Beach was "too calm" for him.

The Palmer-Locke match was a contrast in golfing styles. Arnold outhit little Bobby by fifty and sixty yards off every tee, but Bobby, as is his custom, kept draining putts from everywhere. On the par-five second hole, for example, Palmer crushed a drive about three hundred yards, then smoothed a four-iron to the green, and rolled a 30-foot eagle attempt close enough for a gimme birdie. Locke smacked his tee shot only about two hundred and thirty-five yards, drove a three-wood about seventy yards from the pin, maneuvered his wedge approach to within about 22 feet of the hole, and then dropped his putt cleanly into the middle of the cup. Palmer looked stunned. It was that way all round. Locke would inspect the hole, take two practice swings of his putter, step forward, and with his inside-out stroke roll in one long putt after another. As a result, Arnold and Bobby were all even going to the seventeenth hole, that monstrous par three. Palmer yanked a one-iron over the bunkers and onto the left side of the green, where the pin was set. Locke tried to go the same way with his three-wood, but unfortunately, Bobby's ball plugged against the lip of the bunker, and he was barely able to extricate his ball from the sand. Palmer charged to within a few inches of the cup for a gimme three, leaving pressure on Locke, to make a 45-footer with at least three distinct breaks. Bobby surveyed the putt and stroked the ball as always. For a long second it appeared that Locke had saved himself once again, but at the last moment the ball slid just to the right of the cup and stopped on the edge. Thus, Palmer took a one-up lead to the eighteenth tee, and he won the match by that score as they matched birdies on the final hole. "Bobby," Arnold said as they shook hands, "could I borrow your putting stroke for a few years?" Locke laughed. "Tell you what, Arnold," he said. "I'll give you my putting stroke if you'll give me about fifty yards from your tee shots."

The Sarazen-Boros match apparently was highlighted by Boros's sighting of a giant shark out in Carmel Bay off the seventh green. They both played somewhat sloppily, particularly Boros, who seemed to quick-hit too many of his important putts. Sarazen shot a three-over-par 39 on the front nine but still took a three-up lead on Boros. He closed out Ol' Julius 5-and-4 on a bogey, yes a bogey, on the fourteenth hole while Julius kept hitting balls into people's backyards.

In the bottom half of the draw, Walter Hagen somehow survived half of Pebble Beach's bunkers, the Pacific Ocean, three backyards, two dirt roads, and a minor hangover in edging Harry Vardon 2-and-1. Sir Walter impressed Harry immediately when he holed his fried-egg bunker shot for a winning birdie three at the first hole. Hagen seemed to lunge at the ball in that bunker, but, as he said later, he always lunges at the ball in bunkers. Hagen drove into Carmel Bay on both the fourth and the ninth holes; deposited approach shots in bunkers at the third, eighth, tenth, thirteenth, fifteenth, and sixteenth holes; hit out of bounds not once, not twice, but three times at the par-five fourteenth; and twice landed on cart paths. Playing confidently, almost recklessly, he kept blasting out of the bunkers for tap-in pars, and on those rare occasions when he kept the ball in safe play on a hole, he usually made birdie. For instance, when Hagen took a 1-up lead to the sixteenth, he saved his margin with a marvelous bunker explosion to within six inches of the cup. Vardon just shook his head. Then on the seventeenth, Hagen terminated the match with a terrific birdie two after his four-wood tee shot stopped practically dead against the flagstick.

Byron Nelson was apparently in a bad mood when he went off to play his match against Bobby Jones. Byron played poorly all day, losing 3-and-2 to Jones, who played precisely if not quite spectacularly. Bobby made 16 straight pars. He hit all 12 fairways and 15 of 16 greens, missing only the eighth, where his long approach carried past the green and settled in the knee-deep rough. Nelson tried to counter Jones's almost mechanical consistency with a bold attack, but he kept overshooting greens and missing five-foot putts.

The clock read 12:42, and the WCI was right on schedule as Jack Nicklaus and Dr. Cary Middlecoff stepped onto the first tee. Then it was 1:24 and only Nicklaus had hit his tee shot. The good doctor was still addressing his ball, as he had been for 27 minutes. "Hold it, hold it, hold it," Sam Snead yelled. "Do you mind if we play through?" On the first tee? Fortunately, Nicklaus and Middlecoff, being golfing gentlemen, understood the situation perfectly, so they let Snead and Gary Player tee off and play ahead of them. "Call me collect in Johannesburg if you ever finish your match," Player shouted to Nicklaus and Middlecoff as he jogged down the first fairway.

Snead started off with birdies at the first, second, and fourth holes but was still only 1-up after five, Gary having matched Sam's birdie at the par-five second and won the third with another birdie. Gary then startled Sam on the long par-five sixth hole. Sam hit first and cracked a drive straight down the middle of the fairway about 310 yards. "Catch that," Sam laughed as Gary set his ball on a tee. Gary fixed himself over the ball—arms taut, muscles rippling—and flailed away. Unbelievably, Player's ball passed Snead's *on the fly.* "You little SOB," Sam muttered, looking as if he had just lost his last penny. "How can you do that?" Gary smiled. "If you'd lift weights and eat spinach and drink ninety-nine percent fat-free milk, you could hit the ball three hundred twenty-five yards, too," he chirped deadpan. Gary won that sixth hole with a birdie four, but Sam followed with a birdie two at the seventh, regaining his 1-up edge. However, Player then birdied the long par-four ninth hole, rolling in a 55-foot putt from the front fringe after his four-wood approach had hit the top of the bunker and trickled down from the mound. So after nine holes they were all square and, incidentally, both at four-under-par 32.

They played on relentlessly. Player took the lead for the first time with a birdie at the eleventh, but Snead pulled even with a birdie of his own at the thirteenth when his seven-iron approach shot took one bounce, hit the pin, and spun dead less than six inches away. By now Player and Snead had lured most of the spectators from the other matches, and they both drew tremendous ovations as they walked to the fourteenth tee. Gary made a routine par five; Sam scrambled for his, recovering from a bunker and dropping a 12-footer uphill along a tricky ridge. They halved the par-four fifteenth, too, hitting the green with their approaches and then leaving their birdie putts about 18 inches short. Snead still had the honor at the sixteenth tee, and he thought for several minutes about how he wanted to play the hole, a very deceptive one. The fairway bends to the right about 250 yards out, and the smallish green is nestled among some tall pines and surrounded by many bunkers, thick and deep grass, and a moat-like ravine. At times the smart way to play 16 is to hit a one-iron off the tee and keep the ball in the middle, avoiding both the left side, with its sand and a blind approach over a forest of trees, and at the same time the right side, with its variety of hazards that often cause the second shot to be played out sideways, or even backward.

After much deliberation, Snead—to the amazement of all—took out his driver. Sam obviously wanted to fade the ball down the right side of the fairway, but he blocked out and pushed the ball well off to the right, behind a cluster of trees. He knew that he would have no shot for the green from there. Gary reached into his bag for his one-iron, then drilled the ball straight down the fairway. Sure enough, Snead had to attempt a safety shot, and he left his first recovery in the rough. He played his third shot out into the fairway, a few yards behind Player's ball, and finally lofted a six-iron onto the green about thirty feet from the pin. Sam was on the green in four, madder than Woody Hayes after an Ohio State fumble. Player did not take any chances. He, too, hit a six-iron for the middle of the green, and the ball stopped about twenty feet away. Sam missed his first putt, then, unbelievably, scuffed the tap-in past the hole and took a seven. He told Gary to pick up his ball. Player nursed his 1-up lead by making a routine par three at the seventeenth while Sam was getting up and down from the bunker to the right, then Gary birdied the par-five eighteenth from thirty feet and promptly conceded Sam's twenty-five footer for a birdie. It was a superb match.

To the surprise of most people, Nicklaus and Middlecoff did finish their round. Of course, they finished mainly because Jack gave the doctor the early novocaine treatment, wiping him out 6-and-5 after the thirteenth hole. Nicklaus was six under par for those 13 holes and had an eagle three at the par-five second. "I wish I could save some of those birdies for another day here at Pebble Beach," Nicklaus mused. "Someday when I need them I'll probably shoot an eighty-two or something and lose the Crosby on the last day."

So now it was off to St. Andrews in Scotland for the quarterfinals: Hogan against Trevino in a match between Texans, Palmer against Sarazen, Hagen against Jones, and Nicklaus against Player. We called the quarterfinalists together for a quick meeting at the Del Monte Lodge. "The next round is set for Saturday, July the fourth," we said. Palmer wanted to know why we couldn't play it on Sunday, July 5. "St. Andrews is always closed on Sunday, Arnold," we said. "Remember what old

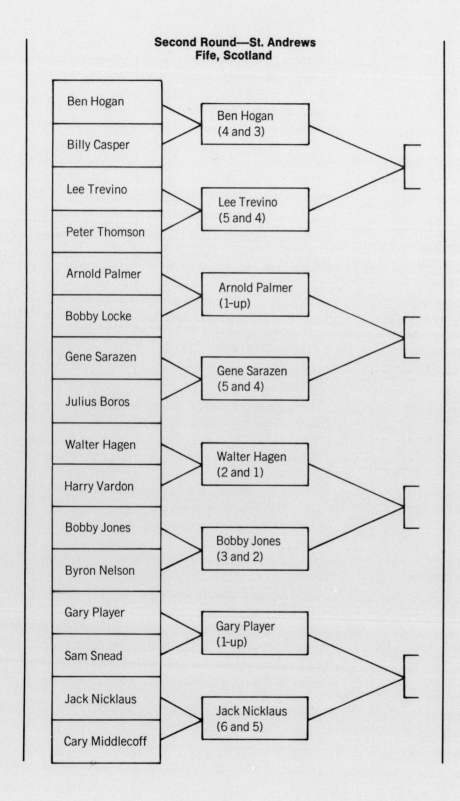

Second Round—St. Andrews
Fife, Scotland

Ben Hogan
Billy Casper
→ Ben Hogan
(4 and 3)

Lee Trevino
Peter Thomson
→ Lee Trevino
(5 and 4)

Arnold Palmer
Bobby Locke
→ Arnold Palmer
(1-up)

Gene Sarazen
Julius Boros
→ Gene Sarazen
(5 and 4)

Walter Hagen
Harry Vardon
→ Walter Hagen
(2 and 1)

Bobby Jones
Byron Nelson
→ Bobby Jones
(3 and 2)

Gary Player
Sam Snead
→ Gary Player
(1-up)

Jack Nicklaus
Cary Middlecoff
→ Jack Nicklaus
(6 and 5)

*If golf wasn't invented here at St. Andrews Old Course, it is properly revered—
an appropriate setting for the second round of the World Classic Invitational.*

Tom Morris once told a golf nut who wanted to play the Old Course on a Sunday: 'The Old Course needs a rest on the Sabbath, sir, even if you don't.' "

On our way to St. Andrews we stopped off in London for a couple of nights on the town. As it turned out, we fairly limped into St. Andrews.

Most people don't know that St. Andrews is, like Pebble Beach, Dyker Beach, Rancho Park, and Ponkapoag, a public course. All you have to do is walk up to the starter's wicket, pay your greens fee —a pound or two—and then play away. Besides the famed Old Course, where the game was really invented, there are a number of other courses at St. Andrews, including the New, the Eden, and the Jubilee, and during the 11-month golf season (nobody plays there in March) more than 250,000 rounds are played on these links. The British Open has been conducted at St. Andrews—always on the Old Course, mind you—21 times, and among the winners have been Jack Nicklaus, Bobby Jones, and three of our first-round losers, Sam Snead, Peter Thomson, and Bobby Locke.

The Old Course is a narrow links, a 6,951-yard, par-72 layout where half the holes play away and the other half play back. In fact there are seven enormous "double" greens. The second and sixteenth holes share the same green, as do the third and fifteenth, the fourth and fourteenth, the fifth and thirteenth, the sixth and twelfth, the seventh and eleventh, and the eighth and tenth holes. The players must contend with such unusual hazards as the Beardies, the Cat's Trap, Walkinshaw's Lion Mouth, the Elysian Fields, the River Eden, the Firth of Forth, a railway line, the Swilcan Burn, and of course, the fabled Valley of Sin. Good luck, men.

Luckily, we encountered good weather for our quarterfinals; none of our players needed more than two sweaters at the start. As at Pebble Beach, the weather conditions at St. Andrews can change by the minute, though, so all the players stuffed

"What a contrast: Hogan,
who says hello and
good-bye but not much
in between, and Trevino,
who says hello and
good-bye and never shuts
up in between. . . ."

their golf bags with velours, rain gear, umbrellas, spare golf gloves, stickum for their grips, and enough towels to keep the London Hilton supplied for a month. "I feel like a mummy," Lee Trevino cracked on the first tee as he walked over to shake hands with Ben Hogan. "Nice day," Hogan said solemnly. What a contrast: Hogan who says hello and good-bye but not much in between, and Trevino who says hello and good-bye and never shuts up in between. Would Trevino throw a rubber snake at Hogan's feet, as he did before his 1971 U.S. Open playoff against Nicklaus at Merion? "If he does," said a Hogan man, "Ben'll wrap it around Trevino's neck and there'll be one dead Mexican in Scotland."

Trevino played it more or less straight throughout the round, especially when Hogan was within earshot. Oh, on the first tee, after Lee followed Hogan's perfect drive with his own perfect shot down the middle, he responded to the cheers from the gallery by shouting, "Folks, I've won two U.S. Opens and two British Opens. What do you expect from me, ground balls?" But when Hogan failed to crack a smile, Lee decided not to waste his quips on the unappreciative. Then Bantam went to work. He birdied the first hole, dropping a twenty-five-footer through a swale while Trevino was scrambling for a par, then went 2-up with another birdie at the short third, where his mid-iron approach practically rolled dead against the flagstick.

As always, Hogan played meticulously, hitting his tee shots to exact positions and dropping his pitches within good putting range. On the other hand, Trevino had driving troubles, hitting his tee shots into the thick gorse, from which only the Nicklaus-type players, with high, upright swings, can hope to extricate the ball consistently. Hogan went 3-up at the ninth when Trevino's tee shot was down so deep into the rough that Lee could hardly see it. Spotting Hogan a 3-up lead is like sending O. J. Simpson one-on-one in the open field against some three hundred and fifty-pound defensive tackle—the man can't be caught. Ben closed out Trevino on the fifteenth hole, 4-and-3, having played the required holes in two under par. "The man doesn't rattle," Trevino said. "Cripes, he never missed one fairway, and he doesn't have his putting yips yet."

Arnold Palmer played an Arnold Palmer round in his 3-and-2 victory over Gene Sarazen. Poor Arnold. Mark McCormack was around, of course, and he had a film crew with him to shoot Arnold's every move for a documentary he hopes to sell to the British Broadcasting Company. The film guys even had a mini-microphone attached to Arnold's shirt in order to record his every word. Considering the way Arnold played, there probably will be many an expletive deleted from that original tape. If Arnold hit a fairway, no one can remember it. He was knee-deep in the thickets most of the round but, true to character, kept charging ahead with miraculous recoveries and knee-knocking putts from afar. On the sixth green, for instance, Arnold's approach from the thick, wiry rough carried so far to the left that it almost rolled into the cup—the cup for the twelfth hole, that is, not the sixth. The best guess was that Arnold was a minimum of 60 yards, 180 feet, from the hole. So what did he do? As Mark McCormack no doubt has told the world by now, Palmer took a full turn with his putting stroke, brought the putter up around his head, and powered the ball in the direction of the cup, on the other side of Scotland. The ball dropped from sight a couple of times as it passed through Glasgow and Edinburgh, then, as Sarazen watched in wide-eyed disbelief, dropped from sight into the cup! A routine Palmer birdie, folks! Poor Sarazen. Gene had only a six-or seven-footer for his own birdie, but after watching Palmer's incredible putt and no doubt wondering what other miracles Arnold had up Mark McCormack's sleeve, Sarazen missed his own putt badly and, incredibly, lost the hole.

Palmer was 1-up after nine holes, moved 2-up at the tenth, where he finally made a birdie that was not out of Ripley's, and then Palmerized Sarazen and his plus-fours with another staggering flourish at the par-five fourteenth. Catch this: Arnold ducked his tee shot in the direction of the Continent, slashed a recovery clear across the fairway, and then—ready, folks?—holed out a 230-yard one-iron for an eagle three. "This army of yours," Sarazen said to Palmer as they shook hands on the sixteenth green. "Where do I go to enlist?"

In the next match Sir Walter Hagen tried to pull a Palmer against Bobby Jones, but he was not quite up to it this day. Jones kept the ball safely in play all the way around the Old Course while Hagen's drives revisited the spots Palmer's had just left. However, Hagen could not repeat Palmer's amazing recoveries. (Indeed, who could have?) Jones jumped to a 1-up lead at the very first hole when Hagen twice submitted his ball to the Swilcan Burn. Thereafter, Jones relentlessly pressured Sir Walter with a string of pars, twice interrupted for birdies. Jones ended Hagen's struggles at the sixteenth hole, 3-and-2.

Rather predictably, Jack Nicklaus and Gary Player attracted the largest gallery of the day. Nicklaus and Player are the best of friends; in fact, Nicklaus has such great admiration for Player that he named his third son Gary. Player, however, obviously resents the fact that most people think Nicklaus is the best golfer in the world. "Americans always insist that Americans are the best at something, like it's a birthright," Gary snapped. "Just because a guy wins the Memphis Open or the Pleasant Valley Classic doesn't mean he's any better than a player—Gary Player, for instance—who has won a half-dozen South African Opens and a lot of Piccadillys." And so they went out to the Old Course, trailed by a cast of thousands, including about five young Nicklauses and some half-dozen young Players.

Gary immediately took a l-up lead when Nicklaus three-putted the first hole from a measly 10 feet. Jack's first putt, for a possible winning birdie, spun out of the cup and rolled almost four feet away. Then he left the return putt hanging on the lip. "If I had been using the smaller, British golf ball," Nicklaus moaned, "that first putt probably would have dropped." Nicklaus now was on the defensive, an unusual position for him. He had to make an up-and-down par for a half at the second and a sliding 12-foot downhill putt for a half at the third. Then Player went 2-up at the treacherous 470-yard, par-four fourth when he made an easy par while Jack got lost in a bunker.

Nicklaus kept cool, though, and after halving the next four holes he cut the deficit to one at the 359-yard ninth hole, making a two-putt par while Player, who had driven into the rough, flew his wedge approach over the green, struggled to a double-bogey six. They halved the next three holes with pars, too; then Nicklaus pulled even at the 427-yard, par-four thirteenth when he hit a prodigious drive, measured at 365 yards by some members of the sports press, and then pitched stiff to the pine for a conceded birdie. They halved the par-five fourteenth hole after mis-hitting their drives—Nicklaus blocking to the right, Player hooking to the left. Hitting first from the fairway to the green at the 413-yard fifteenth hole, Nicklaus lofted a nine-iron downwind to about 14 feet from the pin, and Player followed with a punched eight-iron that rolled onto the green, actually struck Jack's ball, and stopped even closer to the hole. Nicklaus barely missed his birdie putt as the ball slid below the cup at the last moment. Then Player, who had carefully studied the roll of Jack's ball, unaccountably left his putt on the high side of the cup. No blood!

They moved to the 380-yard, par-four sixteenth, and the advantage seemed to swing to Nicklaus, who followed a thunderous 350-yard drive with a perfectly cut sand wedge approach that left the

Third Round—Oakmont
Oakmont, Pennsylvania

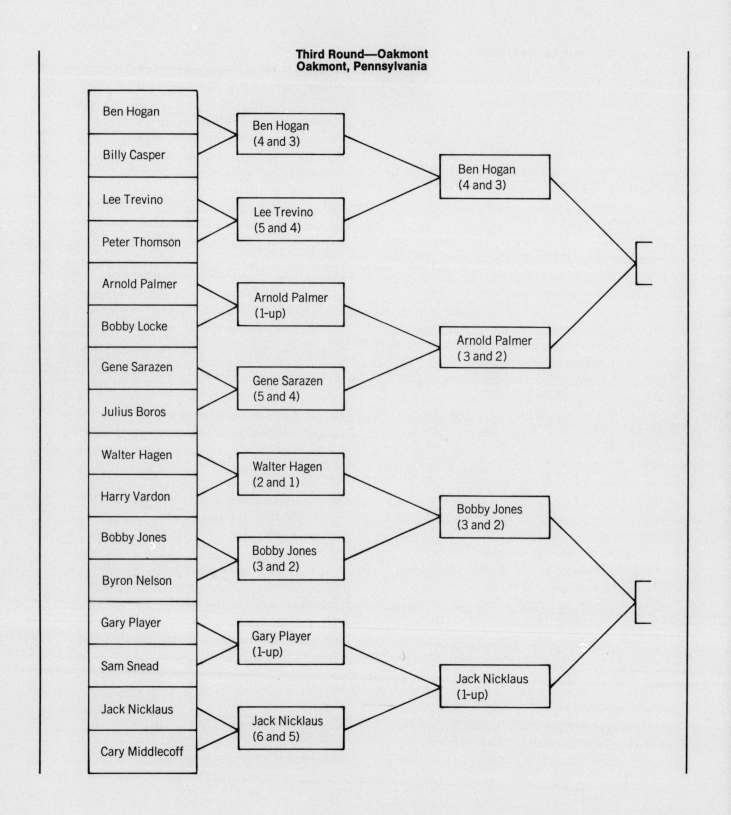

Ben Hogan

Billy Casper

Ben Hogan
(4 and 3)

Lee Trevino

Peter Thomson

Lee Trevino
(5 and 4)

Ben Hogan
(4 and 3)

Arnold Palmer

Bobby Locke

Arnold Palmer
(1-up)

Gene Sarazen

Julius Boros

Gene Sarazen
(5 and 4)

Arnold Palmer
(3 and 2)

Walter Hagen

Harry Vardon

Walter Hagen
(2 and 1)

Bobby Jones

Byron Nelson

Bobby Jones
(3 and 2)

Bobby Jones
(3 and 2)

Gary Player

Sam Snead

Gary Player
(1-up)

Jack Nicklaus

Cary Middlecoff

Jack Nicklaus
(6 and 5)

Jack Nicklaus
(1-up)

ball less than three feet from the hole. Player had pulled his drive to the left and had half-skulled his second shot onto the green some sixty feet from the cup. With disaster staring at him, Gary calmly rolled his putt into the cup and suddenly made Nicklaus feel as though his little straight-in three-footer was a twenty-five-footer with a quadruple break. No matter, Nicklaus rapped the ball into the back of the cup.

At the 466-yard par-four seventeenth, Player again escaped from potential disaster, this time blasting from a bunker and running in a slick twelve-foot putt for a halving par as Nicklaus made a routine four. So it all came down to the eighteenth hole, the great 358-yard finishing hole of the Old Course.

Charged up now, Nicklaus started to undress on the tee. He removed one sweater, then another, and now he was wearing only a long-sleeved turtleneck shirt with his corporate Golden Bear sewn on the front. Then he removed his driver

from the bag. Jack addressed his MacGregor Tourney for what seemed like an eternity and then, with a whooosh, air mailed the ball toward the green. As the gallery gaped, Jack's ball flew across the Valley of Sin, that deeply recessed crevice that swallows golf balls in front of the eighteenth green, landed on the front edge of the putting surface, then rolled ever so slowly toward the pin, finally stopping less than 15 feet away. Jack put his sweaters back on and acknowledged the cheers from the throng.

Player had really no choice. He, too, had to try to drive to the green. Unfortunately, Gary's ball didn't carry the Valley of Sin and, instead, settled at the bottom of the hollow. He had to play a high pitch shot, and the ball failed to clear the mound in front of the pin. So Player was on the green in two, about 45 feet from the pin whereas Nicklaus was less than 15 feet away in one. Player gamely tried to sink his putt, but the ball rolled almost five feet past the cup. Nicklaus surveyed his putt from all

Long enough to require strength, strategically bunkered to demand accuracy, and with a tricky, fast green, the eighteenth hole at Oakmont typifies the challenge of the course.

angles. He could two-putt and still win. Not Nicklaus. He stroked the ball perfectly. It gradually turned toward the cup and dropped in. Another thunderous ovation. Even Player cheered. They had fought each other for eighteen holes, and Jack had won the match 1-up, with an eagle no less on the very last green.

"You won, Jack, congratulations," Gary said as they shook hands.

"We both won, Gary," Jack said.

So, on to Oakmont, for Palmer against Hogan and Nicklaus against Jones in the semifinals.

Let's say it right here: On any given day there is no better golf course in the United States than Oakmont, where the USGA has conducted some eleven National Championships and the PGA two of its championships. In the old days the Oakmont members used to arrive at the club by mule-drawn buckboard from the trolley stop down the hill, but now most of them pull up in chauffered limousines or even helicopters. Oakmont is famous for its lightning-quick greens and its 187 bunkers. "At Oakmont," Hogan said, "you never want to land on the wrong side of the green. You hit the ball to the exact spot on a certain side or else." At least some of the bunkers are unavoidable, particularly around the church pews at the third hole—eight grassy ridges set through the sand. The church pews at the par-four fifteenth and also that 130-yard-long bunker at the eighth might be accused of entrapment. Good luck, men.

Hogan arrived at Oakmont before the other semifinalists and played five more practice rounds than his opponent, Arnold Palmer, who lives up the road in Latrobe and has played Oakmont as often as some members. What Hogan worried about most was Arnie's Army, which is headquartered outside Pittsburgh. "There'll be twenty-five thousand people following our match," Hogan said, "and twenty-four thousand nine hundred and ninety-nine of them will be cheering for Arnold. The only person for me will be my wife, Valerie."

We tried to comfort Hogan by reminding him that he had won the 1953 Open at Oakmont and that Nicklaus had beaten both Arnie and his Army at Oakmont in a playoff for the 1962 U.S. Open. "You're right, I guess," Ben said. "Good golf will win out."

Which it certainly did in the Hogan-Palmer confrontation, the first of our 36-hole semifinal matches. Hogan graciously allowed the local favorite to hit first, and Arnold cracked a perfect drive down the first fairway. Well, Arnie's Army roared for about four minutes, but it could not unnerve the unflappable Mr. Hogan. Ol' Bantam drove his ball next to Palmer's, smoothed a three-wood onto the green, and two-putted for a par, taking a 1-up lead that, as it turned out, he never lost. Hogan won the second hole, too, when Palmer buried his approach in a bunker, and Ben took a commanding 3-up lead at the third hole when Palmer went to the church pews for a Saturday service and wound up making a triple-bogey seven.

Almost unbelievably, Hogan and Palmer halved the next 21 holes, matching identical pars on 18 holes and birdies on the other 3. Then, per custom, Arnold staged a rally by winning the seventh and eighth holes of the afternoon round—really the twenty-fifth and twenty-sixth—with back-to-back birdies. He was still only one down as they moved to the thirty-first (thirteenth) tee. On this tricky 185-yard par three Palmer ripped a seven-iron to within three feet of the pin, and the Army whooped it up. Nonplussed by the commotion, Hogan pulled a six-iron from his bag and put his shot inside Palmer's. Arnie's Army cheered, graciously if somewhat more sedately, for Ol' Bantam. Palmer and Hogan halved the hole with deuces, so Hogan retained his 1-up lead.

Although he had led in the match from the start, Hogan could hardly be confident as they moved to the thirty-third (fifteenth) hole, the toughest at Oakmont. The tee shot at the fifteenth is semiblind and somewhat uphill, and the thin fairway, no wider than the breakdown lane of the nearby Pennsylvania Turnpike, turns slightly to the right. The church pews are out there on the left; in fact there are some seven bunkers in the landing area. The green rests in a bowl and is surrounded by some gaping traps, including a right-side bunker that is almost 100 yards long and about 15 yards wide. Some of the best players in the world have done time there. (In 1953, Hogan played the fifteenth hole in three over par but still managed to win the U.S. Open.) Ignoring the obstacles, Palmer drove his ball longer than he had all day and carried the bend in the fairway with yards to spare. Hogan wisely decided not to risk attempting such a prodigious clout and, instead, drove safely into the fairway. His next shot, though, was inevitable. He hit maybe the greatest three-iron ever played, a perfect hook that soared over the sands of Oakmont and came to rest about four feet from the cup. Apparently, Hogan's shot depressed Palmer, because Arnold's lofted approach fell short, some 50 feet from the cup. Arnold struck his first putt boldly but ran it 10 feet past the hole, then missed his second putt, too. Hogan calmly stroked his ball into the center of the hole, going 2-up to the sixteenth hole.

There was little that Palmer could do now. Miracle comebacks rarely happen against a man of the tenaciousness of Ben Hogan. As Arnie's Army watched with a quiet respect, Hogan closed out their general 3-and-2 on the sixteenth green when he two-putted for an easy par while Arnold was three-putting from somewhere out around Latrobe.

While Hogan was disposing of Palmer, Jack Nicklaus treated Bobby Jones to a golf clinic. Jones won the first hole against Nicklaus when Jack three-putted from 25 feet, but then he mostly played spectator the rest of the game. Nicklaus has rarely played better. He stormed to a 5-up lead during the morning round, shooting a lethal

six-under-par 65, with seven birdies after that lone bogey at the first hole. Nicklaus drove the ball perfectly, outdistancing Jones by 30 and 40 yards off every tee, and whereas Jones had to work long iron approaches over the bunkers to the tricky, tight pin placements, Nicklaus found himself in good position for short lofts over the bunkers. In fact, Nicklaus's longest birdie putt was only 18 feet, and three times he dropped birdies from inside six feet. "It was an awesome display," Jones remarked during the lunch break. Although Jones was Nicklaus's idol when Jack was growing up in Columbus, the Ohio strong-boy showed him no favor on the afternoon round, either. Jack won the nineteenth (first) hole with another birdie, this time with a long—for Jack, that is—30-foot putt. Soon it was all over, Nicklaus having scored a decisive 7-and-6 victory over Jones. He had played the 30 holes in 10 under par. "Jack, as I said once before," Jones said during the handshake, "you play a game with which I am unfamiliar."

So, now here we were, heading across the state of Pennsylvania to crusty old Merion, where Ben Hogan of Fort Worth, Texas, would play Jack Nicklaus of Columbus, Ohio, over 36 holes for the championship of the World Classic Invitational and, of course, for the stately sum of $1 million. Let's contemplate Merion for a moment. Its most distinctive feature is its modest length, compared to many of the other great courses. The east course measures only 6,498 yards and plays to a par at 70. They may be, however, the toughest 6,498 yards in golf. Herbert Warren Wind once wrote, "It takes brains to play Merion. You can't just slug away off the tees, for almost every one of the fairways has a little twist to it, if not a sharp dogleg bend, and you have to place your drive artfully to keep it out of the rough and set yourself up so that you have an opening to the green on your approach shot. The greens are wonderfully varied—plateau greens, bench greens, crown greens, sunken greens, large greens, small greens,

"... Jack Nicklaus treated Bobby Jones to a golf clinic.... 'Jack, as I said once before,' Jones said during the handshake, 'you play a game with which I am unfamiliar.' "

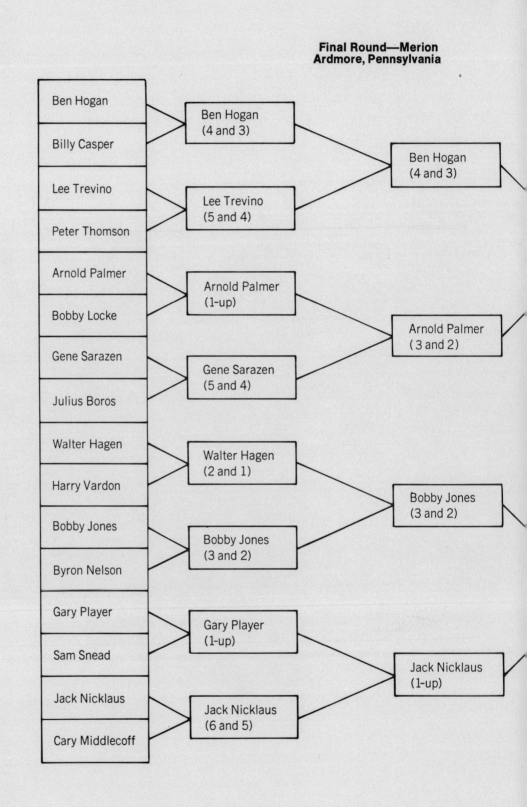

Ben Hogan

Billy Casper

Ben Hogan
(4 and 3)

Lee Trevino

Peter Thomson

Lee Trevino
(5 and 4)

Ben Hogan
(4 and 3)

Arnold Palmer

Bobby Locke

Arnold Palmer
(1-up)

Gene Sarazen

Julius Boros

Gene Sarazen
(5 and 4)

Arnold Palmer
(3 and 2)

Walter Hagen

Harry Vardon

Walter Hagen
(2 and 1)

Bobby Jones

Byron Nelson

Bobby Jones
(3 and 2)

Bobby Jones
(3 and 2)

Gary Player

Sam Snead

Gary Player
(1-up)

Jack Nicklaus

Cary Middlecoff

Jack Nicklaus
(6 and 5)

Jack Nicklaus
(1-up)

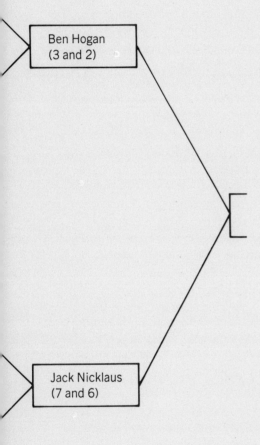

Ben Hogan
(3 and 2)

Jack Nicklaus
(7 and 6)

two-level greens, three-level greens and greens that slope in a hundred different directions.'' Merion lacks only straight greens. The splendid east layout rolls through evergreens, birches, gums, oaks, and elms; curves around creeks and the Baffling Brook; nestles under dogwood; and sprouts daffodils and tulips. It also has its private stock of grass, the famed Merion Blue.

Merion has hosted more than a dozen USGA championships. Bobby Jones began his competitive career at Merion in the 1916 U.S. Amateur. In 1930, Jones completed his legendary Grand Slam there by defeating Eugene Homans, 8-and-7, for the Amateur championship. Back in 1950, Ben Hogan won the U.S. Open at Merion, beating Lloyd Mangrum and George Fazio in an 18-hole playoff that capped his comeback from the horrendous automobile accident that had almost claimed his life the previous year. And Jack Nicklaus mastered Merion in 1960 when he blistered the famed old course with rounds of 66, 67, 68, and 68 for an incredible 72-hole score of 269, 18 shots lower than Hogan's winning total in the Open ten years earlier.

Hogan and Nicklaus both arrived in Philadelphia four days before the championship final. Hogan kept mostly to himself, touring the course as a onesome and playing three and four balls on each hole. Nicklaus had some friends from Columbus, Bob Hoag and Pandel Savic, along with him, and his oldest son, Jackie, joined them in a foursome each morning before Jack returned to the course for some private practice. On Friday night we hosted a small dinner for the finalists down at Bookbinder's. Jack had some Red Snapper that the restaurant had flown in from Florida that very afternoon; Ben stayed with his basic filet mignon swamped with mushrooms. Barbara Nicklaus and Valerie Hogan sat next to each other and had a long chat about needlepoint. At 9:30 Jack and Ben both begged off, saying they needed at least nine hours of solid sleep before a 36-hole match.

Then they returned to their respective hotels.

Saturday was a perfect day, thank goodness. Jack was dressed in a bicentennial red, white, and blue striped golf shirt, navy blue pants and white shoes, according to instructions from CBS control, and Ben was outfitted in his usual white cap, white shirt, gray slacks, and black golf shoes. They both hit practice balls for about twenty minutes and putted for another ten, then walked back to the clubhouse for some last-second freshening up. "I never thought I'd see the day when I'd be playing golf for a million dollars," Nicklaus told a couple of writers. "Who did?" Hogan said. Joe Kadlec, a local hockey celebrity, handled the introductions on the first tee, and Kate Smith sang "God Bless America" as Nicklaus and Hogan stood at attention side by side.

Hogan had the honor on the first tee and played safely down the middle with a three-wood, turning the ball slightly to the right side of the fairway. Nicklaus then took out his one-iron and hit his ball into the edge of the right rough, alongside Hogan's ball. The pin for the morning round was cut right behind the high mound over the bunker on the right side, and Hogan lofted an easy nine-iron over all the trouble to within about 10 feet of the pin. Nicklaus tried to slug a nine-iron from the wiry rough but left the ball in the trap in front. He exploded poorly, missed his par attempt from 35 feet, and then watched Hogan two-putt easily for a 1-up lead. They halved the second hole with par fives, Nicklaus rimming his birdie try from 12 feet, but Hogan took a 2-up lead at the 183-yard third hole when Nicklaus flew his five-iron to the thick rough on the right, below the green and the bunker, then put his first recovery into the sand, and skulled his next across the green and into the rough. Hogan saved a halving par at the 600-yard, par-five fourth hole with a skillful extrication from a greenside bunker, and he escaped with a half at the 426-yard, par-four fifth hole when Nicklaus three-putted down the slope from less than 25 feet.

Nicklaus was playing terribly; for five holes he had made, in order, a bogey, a par, an X, a par, and a bogey. Still, he was only two down. Hogan and Nicklaus both parred the difficult sixth with two-putt par fours, and then Nicklaus finally made his move. Hitting downwind at the 350-yard, par-four seventh, Jack crunched a drive far down the preferred right side and had only a flip wedge to the pin, which was set atop the far level. Hogan, meanwhile, had pulled his drive into the left rough and had to play a safe pitch to the front edge of the green. Nicklaus maneuvered his wedge beautifully, skipping the ball to within 5 feet of the cup. Hogan charged his first putt but it rolled 10 feet beyond the pin, and he missed his next putt, too. Nicklaus calmly tapped his birdie try into the middle, closing Hogan's lead to a single hole.

Nicklaus had another birdie try at the 360-yard, par-four eighth hole but his 12-footer just slid past the right side of the hole. They matched par threes at the ninth and they halved the tenth, too, with bogeys. The tenth is a sharp dogleg to the left, uphill, and they both tried to cut off too much of the fairway. "A bad mistake," Hogan said. "When Jack hit his ball into the rough, I should have played up safe." And so they moved to the eleventh—Merion's famed Baffling Brook—a 378-yard par four. The smart players leave their drivers in the bag at 11 and hit either a three-wood or a long iron down the fairway, which is at a distinct new level at the base of a large hill. Position is the key consideration. If the tee ball lands left, even on the left side of the fairway, you will have an almost impossible shot for the green because of trees, traps, water, and other hazards. If the tee ball lands right, though, the only obstacles are the water—a combination of the slinky Baffling Brook and a moat that rings the green on three sides—and the so-called White Faces of Merion, some of the 130-odd traps that dot the east course. You must hit the green with your approach and keep the ball on it.

And finally to Merion, a short, stimulating test, full of creative challenges, such as the exquisitely contoured and protected eleventh green. Thirty-six holes for the big prize.

Hitting first, Nicklaus played a one-iron for the right side, but the ball kicked right off the hill and bounded into the rough. Hogan followed with a perfect three-wood, cutting the ball into the right-center of the fairway. Nicklaus had a deep lie and tried to remove the ball with his eight-iron, but the wiry rough grabbed the clubhead, turned it, and pulled the ball way to the left, across the Baffling Brook and into the woods. Hogan played a smart eight-iron to the middle of the green while Nicklaus went off in search of his Tourney. He found it lodged against a tree. Jack played a left-handed safety, wedged onto the green, and missed his putt for the bogey. En route to his ball, he picked up Hogan's ball.

Now 2-up, Hogan put more pressure on Nicklaus at the twelfth when he fired his second shot to within birdie range. However, Nicklaus lobbed an eight-iron to about 10 feet, and after Hogan made his 12-footer for a birdie, Jack made his for a half. They matched par three at the thirteenth, then Hogan saved a halving par at the 414-yard fourteenth with a fine shot from the deep bunker at the left of the putting surface and an even finer 12-foot putt while Nicklaus was making a routine four. Hogan preserved his 2-up margin over the next three holes, but Nicklaus won the monstrous 458-yard, par-four, dogleg-left eighteenth with a brilliant four and went to lunch only 1-down. On that hole Nicklaus, normally a fader, hooked his drive into a perfect position at the top of the hill, then slammed a one-iron to the green. Hogan could not reach the green with his three-wood approach, chipped poorly, and then missed his 15-foot putt for the par.

A funny thing happened after lunch. Nicklaus, obviously unhappy with his morning round, went to the practice tee and hit maybe 35 balls to his

faithful caddie, Angelo Argea. Hogan, however, took only a couple of practice putts and a few practice swings with an imaginary ball. So what happened on the nineteenth (first) hole? Nicklaus drove the ball perfectly, while Hogan hit a galloping pulled hook into the deepest rough. Ben had to lay up short; in fact, he was barely able to get his ball airborne. Jack had only a nine-iron to the pin, which now was at the back left side of the green, and he played his shot almost dead to the flag, the ball stopping only three feet short of the cup. Hogan pitched poorly, missed his putt, then watched Jack roll in his birdie, squaring the match after 19 holes.

As played by these masters, the next 12 holes presented probably the most stimulating, most exact, most sensational golf ever. Hogan eagled the 535-yard, par-five twentieth hole, and so did Nicklaus. Jack seemed in a commanding position after booming his three-wood about 255 yards to the middle of the green, about 12 feet from the pin, because Ben had already played up short out of the rough. But then Hogan holed his approach shot from 75 yards, drawing a cheer even from Nicklaus, who then, unfazed, deliberately and patiently surveyed his testing putt and drilled it into the back of the cup. They both parred the 183-yard twenty-first hole. Hogan had the better chance for a birdie but slid his 24-foot putt below the hole. Then they matched birdies at the par-five twenty-second hole (fourth), with Nicklaus again upstaging Hogan, this time with a spinning pitch that stopped inside Ben's nine-iron approach shot, which had carried to within three feet of the cup. Oddly, they conceded each other the putts for the birdie. Now catch this exhibition of long iron play. At the 426-yard, par-four twenty-third (fifth), Hogan slapped a three-iron 10 feet from the hole and Nicklaus followed with a four-iron that stopped about eight feet away. Both made their birdie putts, too. At the 420-yard, par-four twenty-fourth (sixth), Hogan drew a five-iron to within six feet,

"... Ben Hogan of Fort Worth, Texas, would play Jack Nicklaus of Columbus, Ohio, over 36 holes for the championship of the World Classic Invitational and the stately sum of $1 million."

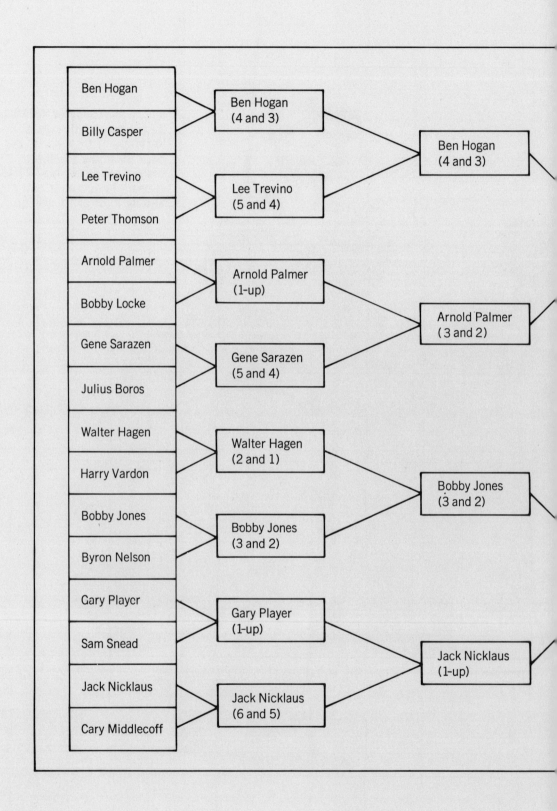

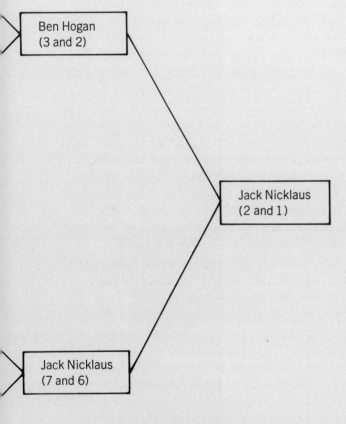

WORLD CLASSIC INVITATIONAL

Ben Hogan
(3 and 2)

Jack Nicklaus
(2 and 1)

Jack Nicklaus
(7 and 6)

First round—Pebble Beach: Monterey, California

Second round—St. Andrews: Fife, Scotland

Third round—Oakmont: Oakmont, Pennsylvania

Final round—Merion: Ardmore, Pennsylvania

but Nicklaus topped him by lofting a seven-iron to about five feet. They both made their birdie putts again. So, over a stretch of five holes, they were both five under par, and over the first six holes of the afternoon round Nicklaus was six under par. And the match was even.

Unable to maintain this birdie barrage, Jack and Ben halved the next four holes with routine pars. Now they were back at the Baffling Brook and, for the umpteenth time in his career, Nicklaus misplayed the hole. This time Jack hit his three-wood, not his one-iron, off the tee, and pulled the ball into the edge of the left rough, leaving himself with only one shot: a safety out in front of the brook. Hogan, per custom, hit his drive perfectly, then plunked an eight-iron to the green. Nicklaus played an inaccurate approach, the ball never quite gaining enough altitude and, as a result, skipping far across the green. Jack two-putted for his bogey, and Ben went back into a 1-up lead, having two-putted a par. "If I never see the eleventh hole again," Nicklaus said, "it will be too soon." Hogan saved his slim lead at the thirtieth (twelfth), canning a downhill, sidehill, left-to-right 12-footer for par after Nicklaus had two-putted for his par from about 22 feet.

For some reason Hogan debated over his shot to the 129-yard thirteenth green. The pin had now been set right over the trap in front, and Hogan apparently could not make up his mind whether to cut an eight-iron into the pin or hit it solidly. What he did, unfortunately, was block the ball well out to the right and into the thick rough beyond the bunker. Nicklaus had no such indecision or unhappy results. Jack lofted a high nine-iron that finally came down hole-high, took a short hop, and backed up to a spot only six feet from the cup. Hogan had really no shot and barely managed to get the ball onto the putting surface, then left his putt short. Nicklaus, taking no chances, lagged his ball to the edge of the cup and tapped it in. So they went to the thirty-second (fourteenth) all even.

Nicklaus now seemed the favorite because the final five holes at Merion definitely favor the long hitter. Sure enough, Jack cracked his longest drive at the 414-yard, par-four thirty-second hole, carrying it far across the rough and way up into the fairway. Hogan, looking a trifle weary, hit his ball crisply, but it was some 40 yards behind Nicklaus's ball in the fairway. Ben maneuvered a three-iron onto the green, but he still had a putt of longer than 50 feet for his birdie. Using a seven-iron, Jack swung easily and cut his ball up close to the pin, perhaps 10 feet away. Hogan made a gallant attempt for his birdie, but the ball went past the hole about 18 inches. Nicklaus surveyed his putt from every possible angle, crouched over the ball, stared at it, and then rolled it into the cup. Jack now had the lead for the first time.

Hogan grittily rescued a half at the 378-yard thirty-third (fifteenth) hole by making a great explosion from a greenside bunker and then canning a tricky 12-footer after Nicklaus had made a standard par, two-putting from 18 feet. But Ol' Ben got himself in trouble at the thirty-fourth (sixteenth) when he pulled his drive into the left rough and had to play his second shot safely, leaving it in front of the quarry. Jack had driven strongly down the right side and, after Hogan hit his second shot, followed with a crisp five-iron across the quarry and onto the middle of the green, some 60 feet below the pin but within two-putt range. Hogan played a masterful shot across the quarry, landing his ball hole-high on the left side, some 15 feet from the hole, and now it was a putting contest. Nicklaus had to get down in two for a certain half, and Hogan had to make his putt if Nicklaus rolled his ball close. Most golf experts have never been able to understand how Nicklaus can drive the ball prodigious distances and also summon a surgeon's touch on the greens. Here Nicklaus baffled them again. He rolled his putt up the hill, through a plateau, and toward the cup. For a moment it appeared as though the ball would continue into the cup, but it stopped just short. Ben had a nasty break between his ball and the cup; he had to start his putt at least four feet above the cup, and if the ball rolled past the cup it might never stop. So he had Nicklaus leave his ball on the green for a possible deflection. Hogan finally putted, but he never gave his ball a chance, leaving it short and below the hole. Dejected now, Hogan shook his head, walked to Nicklaus's ball, and picked it up. So Jack was 2-up with two holes to play.

Nicklaus was unstoppable now. Peering down the seventeenth green, some 225 yards away, Jack stretched his neck and arms, then took out his two-iron. All he did, of course, was hit the ball to the fat of the green about 35 feet from the hole. Hogan, looking really weary, hit his four-wood, but the ball hit the front of the green and rolled back into the huge depression that is Merion's answer to St. Andrews's Valley of Sin. Barring a miracle, it was all over. Hogan chipped to six feet, but when Nicklaus rolled his putt to within about six inches, Ol' Bantam handed his putter to his caddie, strolled over and embraced Nicklaus. "I enjoyed it, Jack," he said. "Mr. Hogan," replied Nicklaus, "I've never enjoyed myself more."

The television announcers, resplendent in their shocking-pink blazers, cornered Nicklaus and Hogan in front of the clubhouse, and we joined the group for the presentation ceremonies. There wasn't much anyone could say. Nicklaus and Hogan exchanged pleasant remarks; the announcers got Jack to agree that the thirty-first (thirteenth) hole was a surprising place for a turning point in any match, let alone the grand final of the World Classic Invitational. Then we gave Jack his check for $1 million. He is the greatest golfer. Ever. "All I can say," Nicklaus said graciously, "is thank you. And let's do it again someday."

"He is the greatest golfer. Ever."

Acknowledgments

Acushnet Company: Dave Branon, Sheila Murphy; *Al Lieber's World of Golf; Apawamis Club:* Frank Cardi, Fred Harkness; *Babcock & Wilcox:* Jim Arens, Dave Birkic; Dale Chambers; *Crooked Stick Golf Club:* Roger Kylie, Marian Richardson; *David Pearson Associates:* Tamara Newell; Alice Dye; Pete Dye; *Firestone Tire & Rubber Company:* Patty Seaburn; *Golf Digest:* Nick Seitz; *Golf Magazine:* Patty Fischer; Ross Goodner; *Gordon Dille Associates:* Gordon Dille; *Habour Town/Sea Pines Plantation Company:* Robert J. Lynn; *Hillerich & Bradsby:* Bennett Curry; *Humphrey, Browning & MacDougall, Inc.:* Phyllis DeLong, Ned Roberts; *John's Island:* Mason Delafield, Charlotte Page, Tom Wilcox; *Kaiser Industries Corporation:* Sue Hayes, Clarice Martin, Vern Peak; *Karsten Manufacturing:* Scott McClellan; *Lloyd & Associates, Consulting Engineers, Vero Beach, Florida:* Betty Agostini; *Lynx Precision Golf Equipment:* Andy Merko; *M. Silver Associates, Inc.:* Ira Silverman; *MacGregor Division, Brunswick Corporation:* Linda Cherry; Stephanie Maze; *Polytechnic Institute of New York:* Lillian Ehrlich; *PGA Tour:* Joe Schwendeman; Wally Phillips; Joe Porter; *Puerto Rico Tourism & Development Company:* Ramona Lopez; Ron Read; *Saint Sam Enterprises:* Sam Barr; *Shamrock Golf Company:* Jack Kirby; Dick Slay; *Spalding, Inc.:* Betsy Bagg; *TaylorCraft, Inc.:* Dave Taylor; *USGA:* Janet Seagle, Bob Sommers, Frank Thomas

Photo Credits

All photos and illustrations by Ellen Griesedieck except:
Acushnet Sales Company   79 all
Babcock & Wilcox   65 top; 66
Paul Barton   39
British Tourist Authority   234–35
Crooked Stick Golf Club   55 top
Melchior DiGiacomo   16 bottom; 135; 139; 150 all; 175 top; 207
Jim Flores   2–3; 93 bottom; 101 all; 113 top left; 122; 138;
          155 left; 158–59; 159 top; 180; 186 left and right; 188–89;
          201 all; 202 bottom
Golf Magazine   32; 50 all
Gordon Dille Associates, Inc.   65 bottom
Harbour Town/Sea Pines Plantation Company   55 bottom left and right
Hillerich & Bradsby Company, Inc.   62–63; 72; 72–73
John's Island   49 all, 54
Kaiser Industries Corporation   88
Karsten Manufacturing Corporation   76 top right
Lloyd & Associates   56-57
Lynx Precision Golf Equipment   76 bottom; 81 all; 84; 85
MacGregor Division, Brunswick Corporation   70 all; 71 all
Moe Incorporated Graphic Design   76 top left
Stephanie Maze, San Francisco *Chronicle*   109 top left; 124; 125
Pinehurst Hotel & Country Club   42; 43 all
Polytechnic Institute of New York   82; 83
Puerto Rico Tourism & Development Company   28; 29 top
Saint Sam Enterprises   77 left
Shamrock Golf Company   69
TaylorCraft, Inc.   77 middle and right
Tony Tomsic   11 top left and right; 168 bottom left; 178 right;
          186 middle; 189; 191; 196 bottom right; 205
United Press International   27 bottom left and right; 129; 132 top right; 133;
          136 all; 140 top; 141; 148; 149; 173; 217 left; 218; 219; 220;
          221 top; 222; 223; 224; 226; 228 left
United States Golf Association 27 top; 31 all; 34–35; 35 all;
          36–37; 215; 241; 247
University of Alabama 132 top left
World Golf Hall of Fame, Pinehurst, NC   30 top
Wide World   30 bottom; 108; 116–17; 117; 119; 132 bottom;
          157 all; 216; 217 right; 228 right